A History of Boalsburg, Oak Hall, and Linden Hall, Pennsylvania

1770-1975

Why They Developed the Way They Did

by Randolph Thomas

© 2020 Horace Randolph Thomas

Printed in the United States of America

All rights reserved. This publication is protected by Copyright, and permission should be obtained from the publisher prior to any prohibited reproduction, storage in a retrieval system, or transmission in any form or by any means, electronic, mechanical, photocopying, recording, or likewise.

Published by Mt. Nittany Press, an imprint of Eifrig Publishing,

PO Box 66, Lemont, PA 16851.

Knobelsdorffstr. 44, 14059 Berlin, Germany

For information regarding permission, write to:

Rights and Permissions Department,
Eifrig Publishing,
PO Box 66, Lemont, PA 16851, USA.
permissions@eifrigpublishing.com, 888-340-6543.

Library of Congress Cataloging-in-Publication Data

A History of Boalsburg, Oak Hall, and Linden Hall, Pennsylvania, 1770-1975; Why They Developed the Way They Did

by Horace Randolph Thomas
p. cm.

Paperback: ISBN 978-1-63233-256-1
Ebook: ISBN 978-1-63233-257-8

[1. Boalsburg--Pennsylvania 2. Colonial History--Pennsylvania- 3. Centre County (Pa.)--History]
I. Thomas, Horace Randolph. II. Title

24 23 22 21 2020
5 4 3 2 1

Printed in the USA on recycled paper.

DEDICATION

This book is dedicated to my mother and high school history teacher, Virginia Thomas, who taught me the importance and joy of history at an early age.

ACKNOWLEDGMENTS

The author would like to acknowledge the help of these people: Mike Casper, Sharon Manno, Virginia Rainey, Dennis and Beth Ricker, Stan Smith, Johanna Sedgwick, and Lee Stout. Without their contributions, this book could not have been completed.

~H. R. T.

TABLE OF CONTENTS

Introduction	7
Early Settlers and Prominent Citizens	9
Early Roads	19
The Churches of Boalsburg, Oak Hall, and Linden Hall	30
Early Settlements, 1775-1799	40
Birth of American Industry, 1800-1819	50
The Prosperous Years, 1820-1855	59
Transition from Wagons to Motorized Travel, 1856-1913	72
Tumultuous Years, 1914-1975	92
Looking Backward and Looking Forward	106
Bibliography	109
Appendix A: Miscellaneous Maps	111
Appendix B: Timeline	129

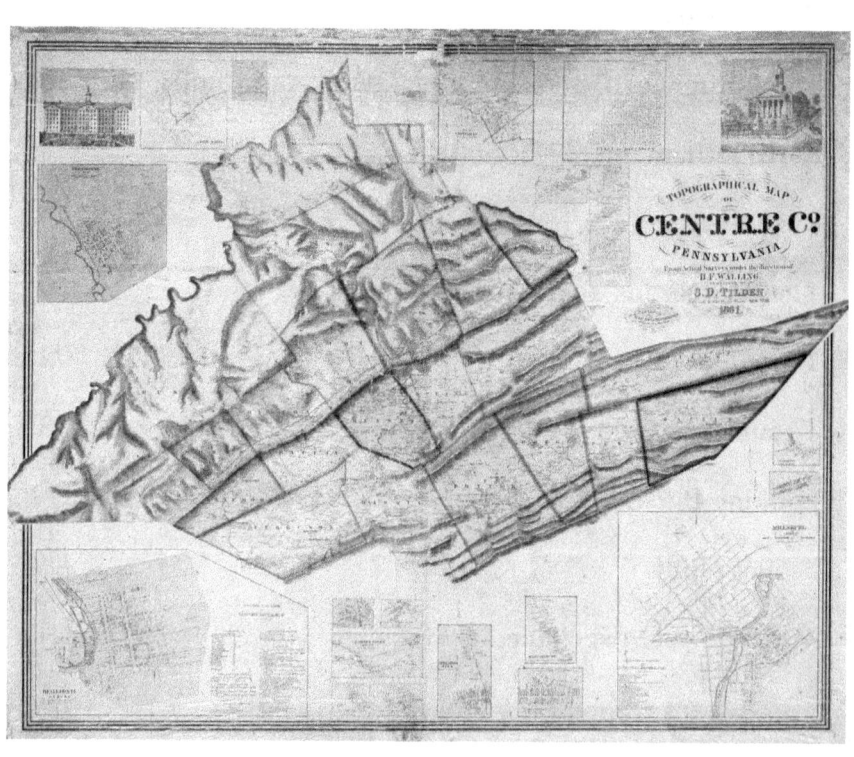

INTRODUCTION

In preparing this history, many sources of information were consulted. Unfortunately, these references often did not cite dates and tend to be incomplete, imprecise, contradictory, or inaccurate. The challenge to the author was to assess the reliability of various sources and to reconcile the sources into one clear, consistent, and accurate narrative that is also consistent with relevant events of American history.

In gathering information and facts for this book, the author has used only reliable sources, and where necessary, conflicting dates have been selected to be consistent with events in American history occurring at that time. Facts that are obviously wrong, legends, and tales have not been repeated.

There have been numerous histories written about Centre County. Many of these writings have focused on the metropolitan areas and the iron industry. Few histories have been written about the rural areas of the county. This is the story of the rural areas of Boalsburg, Oak Hall, and Linden Hall. The factors contributing to their development similarly affected most of the county.

Throughout history, Boalsburg, Oak Hall, and Linden Hall have been linked, both culturally and economically. This book describes the development of these three villages and how their development was affected by external events.

The next three chapters are general and contain information that is pertinent to the region as a whole and are not written chronologically. The following chapter describes the very early settlement of the region and includes a brief biography of some of the more prominent citizens of the three-village region. Their names are readily recognizable. The following chapter describes the network of roads in the region in the early 19th century. A network of roads allowed hamlets to grow into villages and businesses to prosper. The growth of villages is paralleled by the number of churches in the villages. So, the last general chapter describes the churches in the three villages. These three chapters are followed by five chapters that describe the chronological development of the three villages. There was early growth and commerce followed by the birth of American industry. This was followed by a period of prosperity for the region. The period 1855-1975 was difficult. America fought six wars. Additionally, there were two stock market crashes, a pandemic, the Great Depression, and the Cold War. There was little opportunity for local leaders to think about growth issues.

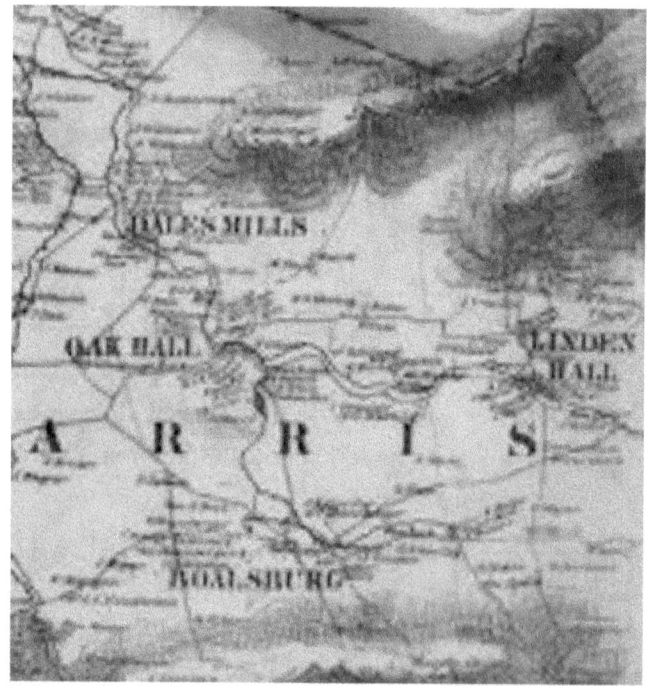

The Boalsburg-Oak Hall-Linden Hall region.

EARLY SETTLERS AND PROMINENT CITIZENS

Early Settlers

The earliest settlers of America moved from the east coast west into the valleys after the Revolutionary War. General James Potter, was the first to record his exploration of the area that would later become Centre County. He followed the West Branch of the Susquehanna River from Sunbury to Bald Eagle Creek in 1759. At the junction of Bald Eagle Creek and Spring Creek, Potter headed south reaching the approximate location where Bellefonte is located today. There he headed east. He continued along an Indian trail, perhaps following Logan Branch, to the base of Nittany Mountain and crossed over the mountain, probably at Black Hawk Gap just east of Pleasant Gap. When he overlooked Penns Valley for the first time, he is reported to have said to his traveling companion, "My Heavens, Thompson, I have discovered an empire." Through an accumulation of warrants and grants, he acquired much of that empire.

The first permanent white settler in Centre County was Andrew Boggs, who settled in present-day Milesburg in 1769, only ten years after the area was first explored by Gen. Potter. The earliest settlements in Centre County were along Bald Eagle Creek and Penns Creek. Harmony Plantation (in present-day Boalsburg) was probably warranted or surveyed in 1766 by Thomas Poultney, and in 1774

Benjamin Poultney built a log home there just southeast of what is now the Boalsburg Heritage Museum and just east of what would become known as Springfield, later renamed Boalsburg. Benjamin Poultney is the earliest known settler of Springfield. The log home of Gen. James Potter was built near Old Fort in 1774. Potter's Fort was built in 1777 by Gen. Potter as a refuge for the settlers of the upper Penns Valley from the American Indians. By 1785, the American Indians had vacated Centre County.

After the Revolutionary War in 1783, more settlers began to migrate westward to Centre County, especially German and Irish emigrants. David Boal, Sr. settled in Springfield in 1789, 15 years after Benjamin Poultney settled there. Centre Furnace began operation in 1792. The Curtin Iron Works near Bellefonte began operation in 1810. The growth of Centre County is signified by the first Lutheran Church in the County, erected in Aaronsburg in 1794.

Prominent Citizens

There have been many prominent citizens of the Boalsburg—Oak Hall—Linden Hall region whose silent deeds and works have gone unrecorded and are unknown. The importance of their contributions to the growth to the Boalsburg— Oak Hall-Linden Hall area is acknowledged. Some of the more prominent citizens of the region are recognized below.

David Boal, Sr. was born in 1764 in Antrim, Ireland and died in 1837 in Boalsburg. He served the American cause as a captain in the Revolutionary War.

It was the practice at that time for the states to repay soldiers for their service during the Revolutionary War by granting them land rather than paying them money. The state limited warrants to around 300 acres, land speculators and those who wanted to build large holdings of land had to work the system to build a holding as large as 4,000 acres. This was likely how Cpt. Boal acquired ownership of 4,000 acres of land in the Springfield area.

In 1789, Cpt. Boal settled in Centre County, Pennsylvania, on his 4,000-acre tract of land and was one of the early residents of the area. There, he built a portion of the Boal Mansion, although he never lived in the mansion. (Relative to the date of construction, the author assessed the reliability of sources because two dates are citied as when the Boal Mansion was built: 1789 and 1809. The source that cites 1809 is viewed from past experience as being unreliable. That source also provides confusing and erroneous information about Theodore Boal and fails to recognize that there was a David Boal Sr. and Jr. Both were involved with construction on the Mansion. For these reasons, it is stated herein that the first part of the Mansion was most likely built in 1789.)

David Boal, Jr. emigrated to Springfield in 1798 and added onto the Boal mansion, where he resided. He also built the first tavern in the eastern end of Springfield (Boalsburg) in 1804, calling it the Boal Tavern.

George Boal, David Jr.'s son, was born in Antrim, Ireland in 1796 and was a Boalsburg farmer and a practicing attorney in Iowa and Colorado. Upon returning to Boalsburg, he was elected to the Pennsylvania Legislature in 1840. Later, he served as an associate judge of Centre County.

George Boal was very influential in the area. He was a founding member of the Centre County Agricultural Society. In 1853, he was one of the founders of the Boalsburg Academy. His lobbying in Harrisburg was part of the reason the state located the Farmers' High School (now Penn State) in the nearby area in 1855.

Theodore Boal was the son of George Boal and great grandson of David Boal, Sr. He was an American army officer and architect. During World War I, Theodore Boal and his son volunteered in France before the United States was engaged in the war. In 1916, Boal returned to the United States and established the "Boal

Theodore Boal

Troop," a horse-mounted machine gun unit. He was made a Lieutenant Colonel and was awarded the Distinguished Service Cross for valor and the Croix de Guerre in recognition of his service in France.

When his wife's aunt died, his wife inherited the Christopher Columbus family castle in Asturias, Spain. To make his wife feel at home in Boalsburg, he built a beautiful stone structure near the Boal Mansion. He then had the entire contents of the family castle in Spain packed into boxes, shipped across the Atlantic, and set up in Boalsburg exactly the same way that it had been set up in Spain. Today, the stone structure is known as the Columbus Chapel.

The chapel contents date from the 15th century and feature centuries worth of Columbus family history. One of the highlights is a sea chest that was owned by Columbus himself. While it's not known specifically if this chest was on his most famous voyage to America, it's still amazing that artifacts tied to Christopher Columbus can be found in the small community of Boalsburg.

The Columbus Chapel

Christian and Felix Dale were affluent entrepreneurs of Centre County as a result of their enterprises in the milling industry. Christian and his son Felix moved to Centre County from Northampton in 1790. They settled about ½ mile north of Oak Hall and ¼ mile south of Lemont in an area that would become known as Dale's Mills and in 1800 erected a large stone house between Lemont and Oak Hall that would be used as a tavern. They operated the tavern for many years. They began as farmers but soon started a sawmill and gristmill business. By 1805 the Dale family had become rich from their pioneering efforts. The operators of the mills were quite industrious, and they later added a hemp mill to the earlier sawmill and gristmill operations. They also invented several labor-saving devices and mill-related machinery. They influenced the area between Lemont and Oak Hall in three aspects: settlement, transportation and the agricultural industry.

Felix's father, Christian, started the gristmill and sawmill and helped establish transportation routes throughout the county. Christian oversaw the construction of General Benner's road (now

The Felix Dale House

called the Benner Pike), and he petitioned the County Court for a road from Dale's Mills to General Benner's road. This roadway would eventually become an important link to the development of Boalsburg, as it connected the northern and western parts of Centre County to Oak Hall, Linden Hall, and Springfield and then onward to points east.

Felix Dale completed building the Felix Dale House in 1823. It is a two-story, five-bay, Georgian styled stone farmhouse with a gable roof. It features two front entrances with a hipped roof porch. The interior has a center hall plan and features finely crafted woodwork. It was placed on the National Register of Historic Places in 1982.

General James Irvin, a prominent citizen from Oak Hall, in the 1800s, was a Major General in the 10th Division of the state militia and a politician. Gen. Irvin represented Pennsylvania's 14th congressional district in the 27th and 28th Congresses. He unsuccessfully ran for governor of Pennsylvania in 1847. Irvin was also a prominent agriculturalist and ironmaster in Centre County, Pennsylvania. In 1822, he built a brick mill just north of his stone mansion in Oak Hall. It was called the Irwin Mill. The Irwin Mill in Oak

Hall was sold in 1864, and the ownership passed through many hands thereafter. At some point in time, it was converted to a gristmill. Gen. Irwin also built a woolen mill on the southern edge of the village of Oak Hall. He was also part owner of the Centre Furnace.

John Irwin, an Irish immigrant who had moved to Penns Valley in 1794, married James Watson's eldest daughter, Anne. John Irwin built a still house near the head of Cedar Creek in Linden Hall. The still was very successful, and the Irwin family prospered.

John built a gristmill in Linden Hall in 1808 and a mill pond to provide a continuous supply of water. He initially built a log house in Linden Hall near the still. About 1810, he built a brick house on the hill above the mill pond.

John later built many of the mills in Oak Hall. He was active in the iron industry, and he and his son James were part owners in Centre Furnace.

Peter S. Fisher was the pastor of St. John's German Reformed Church on Miller Street, in Boalsburg from 1832 until 1857. He was very liberal minded and was committed to missionary work. As such, he was active in the underground railroad. Rev. Fisher was one of the founders of the Boalsburg Academy in 1853.

Daniel Hess was born in 1818 in Aaronsburg. From his early childhood, he was a member of the St. John's German Reformed Church in Boalsburg. He was a prominent traveling merchant (sometimes

Rev. Peter S. Fisher

called a drummer) in Linden Hall in the mid 19th century and built several structures in the village of Linden Hall. He owned and operated several general stores in Linden Hall. He was instrumental in bringing the railroad through Linden Hall in 1885. He died in 1904 and is buried in the Boalsburg cemetery.

Reuben Hunter (1814-1864) was one of 14 children and a doctor in the Boalsburg area. Reuben's daughter, **Emma Eliza Hunter** (1848-1935), married James T. Stuart in 1875. Reuben Hunter served in the Civil War as an assistant surgeon and died from typhoid fever in 1864. His daughter, Emma, is one of several women credited with starting Memorial Day.

Sophie Keller Hall is credited along with Emma Hunter as starting Memorial Day in 1864. She was a longtime member of the St. John's German Reformed Church.

John Jacob Keller was a long-time resident of Centre County and the Boalsburg area. He was born in 1803. For most of his life, he was a farmer. He died in 1848. One of the stained-glass windows in St. John's United Church of Christ on Miller Street (now N. Church Street) is dedicated to Jacob and his wife, Mary.

Sophie Keller Hall

David Keller, the son of Jacob and Mary, was born in 1818 in Cedar Springs, PA. When David was still a youngster, around 1830-1835, his parents moved to the vicinity of Red Mill in Potter Township. David later bought a farm between Pleasant Gap and Bellefonte and farmed it for 15 years. When that farm was sold, David moved to the old Shinnebarger Farm near Boalsburg. During his life, David farmed, taught school, was a cabinet maker, and traded horses. He later moved to Oak Hall, where David and his brother Henry operated a foundry. After his experience at the foundry, he bought another farm. David died in Boalsburg in 1904. He is buried in the Boalsburg cemetery. He was a long-time member of the St. John's German Reformed Church in Boalsburg.

George McCormick, Sr. was probably the first entrepreneur in Oak Hall. He is known to local history as a miller who was the first settler of Spring Mills before 1800. McCormick's name appears in the Ferguson Township assessments of 1801 (which would have included the Oak Hall vicinity) as owner of a gristmill and a sawmill between the Irwin mansion and the present-day Hanson Quarry. In 1811 McCormick sold a portion of his Oak Hall tract to his son, George McCormick, Jr., and a 132-acre portion to John Irvin, Sr. It is not known if he actually resided in Oak Hall.

Joseph Meyer, of Boalsburg, was a member of St. John's German Reformed Church in Boalsburg. He was an accomplished musician and was probably the first organist of the German Reformed Church in Boalsburg. In 1868, he was largely responsible for the Dürner pipe organ being installed in the St. John's German Reformed Church. It was the first pipe organ installed in Centre County. Mr. Meyer died while playing the organ the day before the organ was dedicated. He is buried in the Boalsburg cemetery.

Joseph Meyer

David A. Stuart, son of William and Ester Stuart, was a farmer in the Boalsburg area, who married Martha Johnston. Together, they had six children.

James T. Stuart, one of David's and Martha's children, clerked for his uncle George W.

Johnston at the Monroe Furnace. He also taught school, and later enlisted in the Union Army in April of 1861. He survived the war, including the bloody battles at Antietam, Gettysburg, and Spotsylvania.

William Stuart (1759-1848) was another prominent resident of Boalsburg. He grew up near Londonderry, Northern Ireland and emigrated to America in 1776. William received theological degrees in the 1790s and was ordained as a Presbyterian minister. He was married to Ester Alexander (1774-1848).

James and Anne Watson owned one of the earliest farms in upper Penns Valley. They resided on Cedar Creek near Linden Hall before 1778. Unfortunately, after several encounters with area Indians, they relocated to Lewistown. Upon their return to Linden Hall, it is thought they built a store and a mill.

James and Henry Whitehill and others in his family came to Centre County and settled at the base of Mt. Nittany in 1789. They were among the earliest settlers of Oak Hall.

EARLY ROADS

The narrative about early roads is complicated by materials that do not contain dates and tend to be incomplete, imprecise, and contradictory. The principal references relied upon to develop this narrative are *Linden Hall Roller Mills* (circa 1960), the Whiteside map (1822), the writings of Horner (2019), Magargel (1938), Thomas (1915), and www.livingplaces.com/PA/Centre_County/Millheim_Borough/Millheim_Historic_District.html.

The evolution of roads was exceedingly important to the development of the Boalsburg-Oak Hall-Linden Hall region. After the Revolution, roads began to be built west of Harrisburg before 1790. At first, most of the roads built in early America were built along American Indian paths and trails, were privately financed, and were often toll roads. The very early roads were built mainly for safety purposes. They went from one farmhouse to another or to a fort. They were mainly paths.

By about 1785, most of the American Indians had vacated Centre County and settlers began producing whiskey, grain, and iron ore products for markets along the Eastern Seaboard. These activities required roads to the exit points from the county. Primary exit points from the county were Coburn and Potter's Mills.

As the production of whiskey waned, gristmills and blacksmith shops were built in Dale's Mills, Oak Hall, Linden Hall, and Boalsburg. Gradually, Coburn was no longer a viable exit point. Paths were improved to accommodate wagon traffic, and roads began to evolve to support commerce. Hamlets grew into villages. Roads began to connect hamlets and villages. As businesses began to develop in the 1790s, roads were further improved to accommodate increases in wagon traffic. It is improbable that businesses like Centre Furnace would have opened without a roadway to get their product to eastern markets.

Soon thereafter, toll roads began to emerge. One of the principal advantages of toll roads was that they were probably better maintained than other roads. Toll roads were the superhighways of the day.

As wagon traffic continued to increase, small businesses began to emerge to cater to and repair wagons. In the early1800s, as villages became connected and roads were further improved, it was practical and possible to accommodate stagecoach traffic. The economy of the village of Boalsburg became largely dependent on wagon and stagecoach traffic. The economy of Oak Hall was dependent to a lesser degree on wagon traffic. Increased wagon traffic necessitated improvements in the roads. Roads now began to connect villages.

Early Travel was Dependent upon Paths

Early travel west of Harrisburg was most likely on horseback or by foot. Clark's Ferry crossed the Susquehanna River, and began operation in 1788. Clark's Ferry connected to the eastern end of the Huntingdon path. One of the earliest toll roads west of Harrisburg was Simpson Ferry Road. It was built in 1792 and connected a ferry crossing on the Susquehanna River at Mechanicsburg to Carlisle.

Travel on paths, trails, and early roads was precarious, at best. According to the writer Myrtle Magargel, the very early road network is described as follows:

> ... *The highways were merely trails, sometimes as being only brushed out with rocks, stones and stumps still standing and full of mud holes making them impassable a great part*

of the time. People hoped for a turnpike like other folks were getting farther south in the state. From Lewisburg to Spruce Creek was the desired route, passing through Boalsburg (Springfield), . . .

Upgrades to road networks were necessary to the development of businesses. The first road upgrades were needed to accommodate wagon traffic. Further improvements were needed to accommodate stagecoaches.

Early Centre County Roads

Magargel described the Centre County roads circa 1800 as follows:

. . . one (road) *from Great Island up Bald Eagle Creek to Milesburg; second, from Howard through its gap in the Bald Eagle Mountain across Nittany Valley and over Nittany Mountain at Hecla to the Sunbury Road in Penns Valley; a third, from Antes (now Curtin) through its gap in the mountains to the south, up what is now Jacksonville road, to Bellefonte, from there through the ridge west of the old toll gate house to Rick Forge, thence through Houserville to Centre Furnaces and southward to Tussey Mountain at Pine Grove Mills; fourth, connecting with the last road running past "Blue" spring and thence around the end of Nittany Mountain through Lemont and Oak Hall to the Sunbury road in Penns Valley; a fifth, up Buffalo Run from Bellefonte, passing to the north of State College* (possibly Gen. Benner's Road), *to the headwaters of Spruce Creek near Balleyville; a sixth, running from the Old Fort southward from the Sunbury road, through Potters Mills over the Seven Mountains to Kishacoquillias Valley; and the seventh, which was the first road to be built in the entire region, from the "Great Plains of Penns Valley at the Old Fort, eastward to Sunbury* (likely the Haines Road).

and by circa 1810:

> *At the time the main post road from Sunbury ran west along Penns Valley through the village of Hubler (now Woodward), Aaronsburg, Millheim and Spring Mills, past Old Fort to Earlysville, which then consisted of a tavern and a few small cottages, and thence around the western end of Nittany Mountain, through Linden Hall, Oak Hall and Lemont, down the Mountain's northern side to Dunlap's Tavern at the Bkie Spring and from there past Logan Furnace to Bellefonte. This highway was the main artery of travel to and from this section from the east, and was so much in use that a post office was established in Earlysville, which was later transferred to Old Fort.*

Travel in the early 1800s was both arduous and slow. It took two to three days to go from Milesburg to Aaronsburg. For a trip from Bellefonte to Philadelphia, if a wagon were used, it took from ten days to two weeks.

According to T. Mitchell, a band of highway robbers known as the "Lewis and Connelly Gang" reached the height of their activities in the early 1820s. They had their headquarters in the Seven Mountains, which was wild and unsettled at the time, with only one road through the area. Repeated holdups induced authorities to intervene. A large posse from Centre and Mifflin Counties was formed to hunt these highwaymen. They were finally captured.

With the "Lewis and Connelly Gang" no longer a menace, plans were made for a turnpike between Lewistown and Bellefonte. If this road passed through Springfield, it would have greatly enhanced wagon traffic through Boalsburg and Oak Hall.

Lower Penns Valley

Reuben Haines of Millheim cut a narrow road from Fort Augusta in Union County through Penns Valley to Spring Mills and on to Potter's Mills (often called the Haines Road). With the exception of scattered American Indian trails, this was the first road to be cut west of the Susquehanna River through central Pennsylvania. This early road was followed in 1787 by an improved road following a parallel route, and in 1810 by a turnpike known as the Buffalo and Penns Valley Turnpike.

Another early road went from the west branch of the Susquehanna River (probably near Lock Haven) through Brush Valley to the Mifflin County line. This road may have passed close to Old Fort en route to Potter's Mills and on to the east. The exact date this road was built is unknown.

Upper Penns Valley

An important early road in upper Penns Valley was the Earlystown Road. It was an extension of Haines Road. As written by D. Riker, from there, it traversed past Old Fort and on to Earlystown, Linden Hall, and Oak Hall, around Nittany Mountain, and then

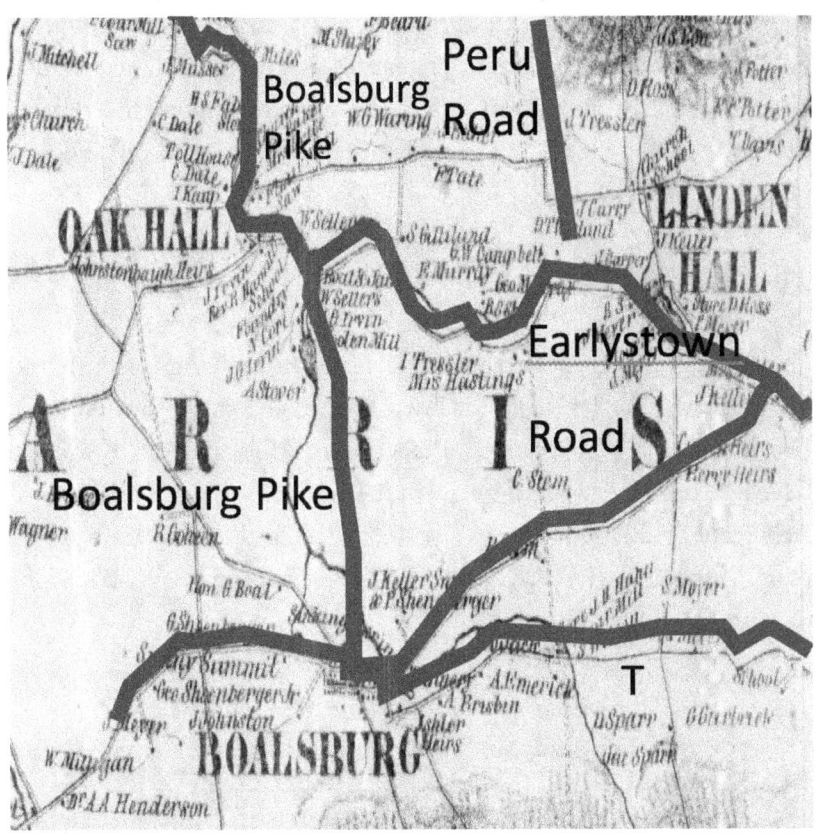

Early road network in the vicinity of Boalsburg-Oak Hall-Linden Hall

connected to General Benner's Road and on to Bellefonte. The exact date this road was built is unknown.

Another important road in upper Penns Valley was Peru Road. This road connected Linden Hall and Peru through McBrides Gap and then on to the county seat in Bellefonte. The date this road was constructed is unknown, but it was probably built sometime after Earlystown Road.

Another roadway of importance to the upper Penns Valley was the Boalsburg Pike. This relatively short road connected Springfield (Boalsburg) to what is now Lemont through Oak Hall. (There is some question about the name of the Oak Hall-Lemont segment of this road, Earlystown Road or Boalsburg Pike as it is called herein. Most early roads probably had no formal name and what they were called evolved over time. Often, a road was likely called different names by different people. Dates of construction would be helpful, but these usually are unavailable.) The importance of this road is that it provided farmers in the western and northern parts of the county with relatively ready access to Potter's Mills, Harrisburg, and beyond.

The Stagecoach Era

As written by C. Horner, one of the earliest stagecoach routes into Centre County was from Lewisburg through Aaronsburg and Earlystown and on to Boalsburg (originally called Springfield). From there, it went through Pine Grove Mills and on to Spruce Creek. Another stage route went between Northumberland and Bellefonte, passing through Linden Hall and along Earlystown road. Mitchell further elaborated on the Northumberland-Bellefonte route, saying:

> *The stage left there* (Northumberland) *at 5:00 o'clock in the morning and was scheduled to reach Aaronsburg by way of the Woodward Narrows, at 6:00 the same evening. It left Aaronsburg at 6:00 the next morning to arrive at Earlysville at noon, reaching John Rankin's tavern in Belle-*

fonte, at the southeast corner of High and Spring Streets, at about 4:00 the same evening.

Further improvements to the Huntingdon path, the Boalsburg spur, and beyond made expanded stagecoach travel possible. The date when stagecoach travel through Springfield began is not known, but it is thought to be around 1804, which would coincide with the opening of the Boal Tavern and the building of the Springfield-Potter's Mills toll road. In 1808, Clark's Ferry became part of a stagecoach line to Huntingdon and Alexandria over the eastern part of the Huntingdon-Cambria Turnpike.

During the 1807 session of Centre County Court, it was confirmed that a 34-foot-wide road would be opened, cleared, and bridged where necessary. It was to run from "the smithy of John H. King and Edward Crouch, continue through the woods to Earlystown Road, on past the east end of John Irwin's house and through his corn field to Watson's mill." This road was to be wide enough to accommodate stagecoach traffic. It is not known if this road was ever built.

Local stagecoach travel in the early 1800s is best described by Magargel:

> *The first ones* (stagecoaches) *seem to have veered south of Boalsburg, taking in Huntingdon on highways already well trodden, but as soon as the multiplying population of Penns Valley made feasible the shorter route* (from Harrisburg to) *Lewisburg and Spruce Creek, it was laid out and traffic began to flow between the east and the west, stopping at the inns that punctuated the way. There were two stage routes to go through Boalsburg. One called the Brush Valley route travelled from Millheim to Spring Mills to Centre Hall to Linden Hall to Boalsburg, thence to Pine Grove past the Pine Stump School house.*

The second way from Centre Hall back to Old Fort, then to Boalsburg through Earlystown and over the road past Whiskey Hollow school house. All roads were dangerous when first laid out and for years afterward. Panthers sometimes sprang from trees upon the travelers and wildcats prowled the woods, hungry and vicious, especially in winter. No less to be feared were the robbers that infested the highways. Men were held up and robbed in broad daylight . . .

Early Boalsburg road sign

Springfield (Boalsburg) became an important hub for local stagecoach travelers and later for cross-state travel. Springfield was at the intersection of several major roadways, was a gateway to the east, provided ready access to Lewisburg and Northumberland, Lewistown, Harrisburg, Bellefonte, and Spruce Creek, and overnight lodging was available.

The local stagecoach road entering Linden Hall passed in front of the John Irwin House, forded Cedar Creek and joined Earlystown Road about a mile away. At this junction stood an inn/tavern and several other buildings. This settlement was called Earlystown. The tavern was one of the earliest establishments in the county along the stage route. The inn/tavern was first recorded on the County tax list in 1808. The inn/tavern was demolished in the 1920s.

The cross-state Philadelphia-Pittsburgh stagecoach route was built piecemeal and came later. On the March 4, 1807, an act in the PA legislature was passed incorporating a company to construct a turnpike from Harrisburg through Lewistown and Huntingdon to Pittsburgh. A

Early stagecoach used for long journeys (Horner 2019)

supplement to this act was passed in 1810 incorporating a company to construct the Huntingdon, Cambria, and Indiana Turnpike. The main stagecoach route would have left Philadelphia and traversed over the Lancaster Turnpike en route to Harrisburg. From there, it would have crossed Clark's Ferry, gone up the Huntington path, traversed over the Huntingdon, Cambria, Indiana Turnpike, and then on to Pittsburgh. The Springfield spur would have intersected this route at Lewistown and maybe at Water Street. It was unlikely this Springfield route would have been heavily used by through travelers. The main route was likely not finished for travel for several years after 1810. The activities of the "Lewis and Connelly Gang" may have also discouraged the use the Lewistown-Potter's Mills-Springfield-Spruce Creek route. A parallel road was also constructed during this same time frame from Ebensburg to Philipsburg in Centre County. The implication to Springfield of this timing is that cross-state travel between Philadelphia and Pittsburgh may not have been possible until around 1812-15.

Toll Roads

Toll roads were very commonplace in early America. An advantage of toll roads was that they were likely better maintained

TOLL RATES

For every score of Sheep or Hogs.	6 cents
For every score of Cattle.	12 cents
For every Horse and Rider.	4 cents
For every led or driven Horse, Mule or Ass.	3 cents
For every Sleigh or Sled drawn by one horse or pair of Oxen.	3 cents
For every Horse or pair of Oxen in Addition.	3 cents
For every Dearborn, Sulky, Chair or Chaise with one horse.	6 cents
For every Horse in Addition.	3 cents
For every Chariot, Coach, Cochee, Stage, Phaeton or Chaise with two Horses and four wheels.	12 cents
For every Carriage of pleasure by whatever be it called the same according to the number of wheels and horses drawing the same.	
For every Cart or Wagon whose wheels do not exceed three inches in breadth, drawn by horse or pair of Oxen.	4 cents
For every Cart or wagon whose wheels exceed three inches and does not exceed four inches in breadth for every horse or pair of oxen drawing the same.	4 cents
Wheels exceeding four and not exceeding six inches.	3 cents
Wheels exceeding six and not exceeding eight inches.	2 cents
All Carts or Wagons whose wheels exceed eight inches in breadth. Free.	

DAVID T. SHRIVER, Supt.

Typical toll rates [circa 1811].

than non-toll roads. Toll rates varied according to weight and wheel width. Centre County was no exception to toll roads.

A toll road of local significance was built in all probability from Lewistown to Potters Mills. The only remains of this toll road are the stone toll house which is on the grounds of Hartman Center, the United Church of Christ summer camp, in Milroy, PA. There was also a toll road from Potter's Mills to Springfield.

With the opening of the Springfield-Potter's Mills toll road, in circa 1804, an alternate route to Potter's Mills was created. The Oak Hall-Springfield-Potter's Mills route was more direct and shorter than Oak Hall-Linden Hall-Earlystown-Old Fort-Potter's Mills. It soon became the preferred route.

The 1861 map of Centre County by Tilden also shows a toll house on Earlystown Road between Oak Hall and Dale's Mills. There was also a toll house in what was to become Lemont. Little else is known about these toll roads.

Sources

The narrative about early roads is complicated by materials that do not contain dates and tend to be incomplete, imprecise, and contradictory. The principal references relied upon to develop this narrative are Linden Hall Roller Mills (circa 1980), the Whiteside map (1822), the writings of Horner (2019), Magargel (1938), Mitchell (1915), and www.livingplaces.com/PA/Centre_County/Millheim_Borough/Millheim_Historic_District.html

THE CHURCHES OF BOALSBURG, OAK HALL, AND LINDEN HALL

The principal references relied upon to develop this narrative are Linden Hall Garden Club (circa 1980), the Whiteside map (1822), the Tilden map (1861), the Nichols map (1874), and the writings of Thomas (1915), Rickert (circa 1980), Rishel (1976), Shortess et al. (1940), and Van Tries (1902).

The first settlers in Penns Valley were Scotch-Irish, and by 1775, there were about 25 families in the upper Penns Valley. These were very devout people. Three prominent early settlers to the area were David Boal, Sr., David Boal, Jr., and John Irwin. They were Irish immigrants.

The Irish settlers were mostly Presbyterians. Many of the earlier churches in the county were also Presbyterian. The German influence began to dominate after 1800. These settlers migrated toward the German Reformed and Evangelical churches. The Presbyterian influence began to wane. In 1957, the German Reformed Church and the Congregational Church merged to form the United Church of Christ. Sometime during the 1955-1970 timeframe, the Evangelical Church was absorbed by the Methodist Church.

Cedar Creek Church

The Cedar Creek Congregation, as it was called, began worshipping in a log schoolhouse (possibly someone's home that served as a schoolhouse) near the head of Cedar Creek. By 1789, the decision was made to build a church, which was to be called the West Penns Valley Congregation. There is strong evidence to suggest that this church was to be a Presbyterian Church. The Church was to be built on ten acres of land given by Gen. James Potter, which was given to the church and was to serve as a cemetery.

As stated by Rickert, before the Church was complete, a dispute arose within the Congregation as to the location of the Church. The Congregation did not survive this quarrel, and the Church building was never completed and was subsequently disassembled.

Sinking Creek and Slab Cabin Run Churches

Part of the Cedar Creek Congregation withdrew eastward and formed the Sinking Creek Presbyterian Church. The date of construction of the original Sinking Creek Church was 1793, when a log structure seating about 200 was built on land purchased from Alexander Johnnston from Centre Hill. Their first pastor was Rev. James Martin. The Sinking Creek Church was one of the oldest churches in Centre County. The church was located along Sinking Creek at the base of Egg Hill in Potter Township. The Sinking Creek Presbyterian Church was also known as the East Penns Valley Church.

A second church was next built in Centre Hill in circa 1795, and the first church built at the base of Egg Hill was abandoned. The Centre Hill building served the congregation until 1842, when the property was sold, new Centre Hill property was purchased, and a brick structure costing about $8,000 was erected. John Irwin of Linden Hall, Gen James Irwin, John's son from Oak Hall, and George Boal of Boalsburg were listed as members in 1852.

The third Centre Hill building was sold in 1887 when the congregation moved to Centre Hall. It has been written by Rishel that "during the 1880s the Sinking Creek Congregation diminished in size as the busy little village of Centre Hall expanded" so those in the Sinking Creek Congregation that were of the 'Presbyterian' persuasion erected a new church building" in Centre Hall in

1888. Another part of the Congregation may have gone to Linden Hall and joined the Evangelical Church. The doors of the Sinking Creek Church in Centre Hill closed in circa 1895. The Sinking Creek Church in Centre Hall closed in 1965.

The remainder of the Cedar Creek Congregation went westward in 1794 and formed the Slab Cabin Presbyterian Church. The Slab Cabin Church was located adjacent to the Spring Creek cemetery and was located on what was at the time known as "Benner's Hill." "Benner's Hill" is the current location of the Centre Hills Country Club. (There is genuine disagreement as to the name of this Church. Rickert (circa 1980) and others refer to it as the Slab Cabin Church. The Presbytery consistently calls it the Spring Creek Church. Since the church was built in the Slab Cabin Creek watershed, it will be called herein the Slab Cabin Presbyterian Church, recognizing that the name may be otherwise.)

The Spring Creek cemetery is one of the oldest cemeteries in Centre County. Gen. Potter's second wife was buried there in 1792. There the congregation erected a log building in 1794. It was not finished until 1802. It was repaired and enlarged in 1832. The church became inactive sometime after 1872.

Branching Out

The Slab Cabin Church was the mother church to three or four other churches, the State College Presbyterian Church, a church in Boalsburg of which no records survive, the Spring Creek Church in Lemont, and perhaps one other.

In 1847, the Slab Cabin Church burned. Part of the congregation favored rebuilding at the same site while the remainder of the Congregation wanted to move to Boalsburg. The Church was replaced with a frame structure at the same site. The Slab Cabin Congregation continued to worship there.

The part of the Slab Cabin Congregation that favored a Boalsburg move probably left the congregation for Boalsburg in 1853 and established a church in Boalsburg. It was never organized as a formal Presbyterian church, although it is called that in numerous writings. They shared a building on Morrison Street with the Boalsburg Academy. The Church used the first floor for worship and the Academy used the second floor. The Academy closed in the 1880s, and in 1892, the building was purchased by the church. The original building was demolished, and a new church building was erected soon thereafter. This second building is still visible today on Academy Street. While this building is often referred to as the "Academy Buiding," it was never occupied by the Academy. Nothing else has been written about this congregation after 1893. In 1957, the building was sold to the Harris Township Lions Club.

In 1888, part of the Slab Cabin Congregation left to form the State College Presbyterian Church. That same year, another part of the Congregation left to establish the Spring Creek Church in Lemont. From 1853 to 1888, the Slab Cabin Church had significant departures. It is unlikely that the Slab Cabin Church could withstand these exits, and soon thereafter the Slab Cabin Church became inactive.

The Evangelical Churches

There is no known connection between the Evagelical Church and the Cedar Creek Church, but nevertheless there is a connection to Linden Hall, as explained below.

By the mid 1800s, it is thought that there were three Evangelical churches in the immeduate vicinity of Linden Hall. There was an Evangelical church in Linden Hall. There may have been an Evangelical church at Oak Hall. The church at Egg Hill was also an Evangelical church. Generally, dates when these churches were built and became inactive are not always known. When the churches in Linden Hall, Egg Hill, and Oak Hall became inactive, their members may have scattered to various other churches in the area.

A church is shown at the base of Egg Hill on the 1822 Whiteside map. It is the only church shown on the map in the immediate area. This church is identified as a Presbyteran church located adjacent to Sinking Creek and is on the road to Linden Hall. This may

The Egg Hill Evangelical Brethren Church, Potter's Mills, PA

have been the abandoned first Sinking Creek Church. On the 1861 Tilden map, an Evangelical Church is shown in the same general location. Nothing is known about this church.

In 1810, an Evangelical class was formed on Potter's Plains. It is thought that this class built a church on a bluff at the edge of Egg Hill in 1837. This church was probably replaced by a new structure in 1860, also located on Egg Hill. This 1860 church is known as the Egg Hill Evangelical Brethren Church. It is thought to have been built by the Sinking Creek Congregation. Services continued there until 1938. This building is listed on the National Registry of Historic Places.

According to Shortess, soon after the first Evangelical Brethren Church was built in 1837, a class was formed and churches were built in Linden Hall and Tusseyville. The location of the church in Linden Hall cannot be established with certainty. Historical writings indicate that only two churches were ever built in Linden Hall. Since the existing church building was built by the Dubsites in 1897, the church described by Rishel along with photographic evidence must be the original Evangelical Church in Linden Hall. It was built on the south side of the road to Centre Hall next to the Rock Hill School. This church was built in 1837. In the early 1880s, this church

The Original Evangelical Church, Linden Hall, PA

became divided into two loosely arranged groups, the Esherites and the Dubsites. In the early 1880s, a dispute arose between the two groups, causing the Dubsites to leave the Church. The Esherites continued to worship in the original building until the early 1900s when the Esherite Congregation became inactive. Over the next 25-30 years, the building deteriorated. It was disassembled in 1933.

Meanwhile, the Dubsites purchased a tract of land on the corner of the John T. Ross lane. There, in 1897, they built a new church across Ross Lane from the original Evangelical building. The new church was built during the height of the economic resurgence in Linden Hall from the logging and lumber operations. It was the second church built in Linden Hall and is still standing. There is no written record of another church being built in Linden Hall. Today, the church is known as the Evangelical Methodist Church and is inactive.

Boalsburg Churches

At one time there were four church congregations in Boalsburg. In circa 1820, two congregations began meeting in the upper schoolhouse in Oak Hall. These were congregations of the German Reformed Church and the Lutheran Church. In 1822, the German

The Zion Union Church (The Old Stone Church), Boalsburg, PA

Reformed Congregation was officially recognized as a denominational church. A year later the Lutherans were recognized as a denominational church. In 1825, the two churches jointly decided to build a church on Miller Street in Boalsburg. The church building, which was dedicated in 1827, quickly became known as the "Old Stone Church." Its official name was the Zion Union Church. It was the first church built in the village of Boalsburg.

Six years after the "Old Stone Church" was erected, the Methodist Church built a church building in 1833 on Pine Street in Boalsburg. This congregation was small and became inactive circa 1872.

In 1860, the German Reformed Church sold its interest in the "Old Stone Church" to the Lutheran congregation for $3.50 and began planning for a church building of its own. In 1862, the German Reformed Congregation dedicated their

The German Reformed Church, ca. 1862, Boalsburg, PA.

new church on Miller Street (now Church Street). This was the third church building built in Boalsburg. In 1868, the Zion Union Church ("Old Stone Church") was demolished due to structural deficiencies in favor of a new Zion Lutheran Church, which was built on the same site.

In 1868, St. John's German Reformed Church installed a pipe organ built by Charles F. Dürner of Quakertown, PA. It was the first pipe organ in Centre County. Joseph Meyer of Boalsburg was largely responsible for the procurement and payment for the cost of the organ. Joseph Meyer died while playing the organ the day before the organ was dedicated. In 1902, the St. John's German Reformed Church underwent a $7,000 remodeling project.

In 1853, a congregation of Presbyterians moved to Boalsburg. They shared a building with the Boalsburg Academy. When the Academy closed in 1893, the building was purchased by the church. The original Academy building was demolished, and a new church building was built. No records survive to record what happened to this church.

The Oak Hall Evangelical Church

In the first half of the 19th century, the Evangelical Church had a strong presence in Pennsylvania. As early as the 1820s, the Albrecht People came to Centre County as a loosely organized church founded by a preacher named Jacob Albrecht. He was an American Christian leader and founder of Albright's People. This group of churches was officially named the Evangelical Association in 1816. These churches underwent various mergers and today is a part of the United Methodist Church. The merger with the Methodist Church occurred in 1967.

The Evangelical Church, it has been said, established numerous churches scattered throughout Centre County. It is further said that eventually there was an Evangelical Church in almost every town in Pennsylvania.

There is no written record of an Evangelical church ever being built in Oak Hall, although the location of an Albright Church is

37

The Evangelical Methodist Church, Linden Hall, PA

recorded on the 1861 map of Centre County by Tilden and in the *Atlas of Centre County* by Nichols (Pomeroy) in 1874. It has been written that "Surely a building was planned at Oak Hall . . ." as there were many Evangelicals living in Oak Hall. Whether a church was actually built or when is unknown.

Possibly the Albright Church, Oak Hall, PA

If there was ever an Evangelical Church built in Oak Hall, as noted on the 1861 and 1874 maps of Centre County, and it still exists, it is probably located on the present-day site of the Oak Hall Hansen Quarry, on the right-hand side of Boalsburg Pike in route to Lemont. Here sits a simple, stone structure that appears to be currently in use by the present quarry operation as an office or as a storage area. It was obviously not typical of a residence.

Sources

The principal references relied upon to develop this narrative are Linden Hall Garden Club (circa 1980), the Whiteside map (1822), the Tilden map (1861), the Nichols map (1874), and the writings of Thomas (1915), Rickert (circa 1980), Rishel (1976), Shortess et al. (1940), and Van Tries (1902).

The first settlers in Penns Valley were Scotch-Irish, and by 1775, there were about 25 families in the upper Penns Valley. These were very devout people. Three prominent early settlers to the area were David Boal, Sr., David Boal, Jr., and John Irwin of Linden Hall.

The Irish settlers were mostly Presbyterians. Many of the earlier churches in the county were also Presbyterian. The German influence began to dominate after 1800. These settlers migrated toward the German Reformed and Evangelical churches. The Presbyterian influence began to wane.

In 1957, the St. John's German Reformed Church and the Congregational Church merged to form the United Church of Christ. Sometime during the 1955-1970 timeframe, the Evangelical Church was absorbed by the Methodist Church.

EARLY SETTLEMENTS, 1775-1799

Some of the more notable local events occurring during the very early years of Springfield (Boalsburg), Oak Hall, and Linden Hall are:

1764—Gen. James Potter is the first non-native to explore Centre County (Linn writes that this date was 1759.)
1765—Provincial land office opens
1766—Thomas Poultney purchases Harmony Plantation in Springfield
1769—Andrew Boggs becomes the first white settler in Centre County
1774—Benjamin Poultney is the first settler in Springfield
1777—Gen. Potter builds Potter's Fort
Circa 1778—The "Great Runaway" to Fort Granville in Lewistown follows a reported incident with American Indians in May 1778
1779—Cleary Campbell becomes one of the first settlers to return from Lewistown to Penns Valley following the "Great Runaway"
Circa 1785—Settlers begin returning to upper Penns Valley after the "Great Runaway"
1785—All American Indians have left Centre County

1789—James and Henry Whitehill settle in Oak Hall

1789—David Boal, Sr. moves to Springfield and is thought to have built the Boal Mansion

1790—Christian and Felix Dale move to Centre County

Circa 1790—All American Indians have left Centre County

1792—Centre Furnace begins operation as the first business in Centre County

1794—John Irwin emigrates to Linden Hall

Circa 1795—The Springfield-Potter's Mills toll road and Boalsburg Pike are built, opening an alternate route to Potter's Mills and the eastern seaboard

Co-Existence with the American Indians

The first permanent white settler in Centre County was Andrew Boggs, who settled in present-day Milesburg in 1769, only ten years after the area was first explored by Gen. Potter. The earliest settlements in Centre County were along Bald Eagle Creek and Penns Creek.

Harmony Plantation (in present-day Boalsburg) was warranted or surveyed in 1766 by Thomas Poultney, and in 1774 Benjamin Poultney built a log home there just southeast of what is now the Boalsburg Heritage Museum and just east of what would become known as Springfield, later renamed Boalsburg. Benjamin Poultney is the earliest known settler of Springfield.

The log home of Gen. James Potter was built near Old Fort in 1774. Potter's Fort was built in 1777 by Gen. Potter as a refuge for the settlers of the upper Penns Valley from Indian raids. One raid, in particular, involved the Standford family and occurred in May 1778. The raids originated primarily from the Ohio River Valley, and were designed to strike terror and drive the settlers out.

The settlers eventually fled in what was called the "Great Runaway." They fled to Sunbury/Fort Augusta, which was an active military post throughout the Revolutionary War.

In 1779, Cleary Campbell was one of the first to return. By the early and mid-1780s, other settlers began to come back. By about

1785, there were no American Indians left in Centre County. In 1789, the James Whitehill family moved to Oak Hall. Little else is known about the Whitehill family. In 1790, the Christian Dale family moved to a farmstead about ½ mile north of what would become Oak Hall and began farming. Eventually, they built a sawmill and gristmill.

Oak Hall tract traces back to a large piece of property surveyed in the warrantee name of Benjamin Bayless, with letters of patent granted to Samuel Wallis. In 1768 Wallis deeded the land to Reuben Haines, who in turn, in circa 1800, sold it to George McCormick, Sr. McCormick's name appears in the Ferguson Township assessments of 1801 as owner of a gristmill and a sawmill in Oak Hall.

Early Liquid Growth

After the Revolutionary War in 1783, more settlers began to migrate westward to Centre County, especially German and Irish emigrants. David Boal, Sr. settled in Springfield in 1789, 15 years after Benjamin Poultney settled there. The early growth of Centre County is signified when the first Lutheran Church in the County was built in Aaronsburg in 1794.

The importance of farming to the early development of central Pennsylvania was due in large part to the Commonwealth's most available resources: fertile farmland, an abundance of streams, and dense forests. The soil and climate of Central Pennsylvania was conducive to grain crops.

Whiskey was a popular drink immediately following the Revolutionary War, and farmers often supplemented their income by operating small stills. Farmers distilled their excess grain into whiskey, which was easier and more profitable to transport than the more cumbersome grain. Cash was always in short supply on the frontier, so whiskey often served as a medium of exchange.

Whiskey was largely responsible for generating revenue in the early years in Linden Hall and the surrounding area. Before circa 1800, much of the local grain was distilled and transported in liquid form. While there were about 6 churches in the area, there were some 40 still houses, and drinking hard spirits was endemic in the area, especially at harvest time. In upper Penns Valley, whiskey was transported via wagon to Spring Mills and to the Forks (Coburn). From there, it was loaded onto arcs and shipped downstream on Penns Creek to Selinsgrove. Wheat and flour were transported overland to eastern markets via wagons consisting of teams of two or four horses, but this option was more costly and time consuming than producing and transporting whiskey.

In 1791-1794, the Whiskey Rebellion occurred. At issue was a federal whiskey tax that it is argued that was applied disproportionately to the disadvantage of small producers. Many producers, especially those in western PA, just refused to pay the tax, so President Washington sent a militia force to quell the rebellion and collect the tax. It is possible that the whiskey tax discouraged local farmers from distilling whiskey. After around 1795, flour and grain became an increasingly profitable form of produce, as is evident from the building of gristmills, specifically the Dale gristmill in Dale's Mills around 1800, the McCormick gristmill in Oak Hall in 1800, and the John Irwin gristmill in Linden Hall in 1808.

Because of the need for grain to be processed, the first businesses in most new settlements were sawmill operations and gristmills. Within the next 30-40 years, the three-village region would support a number of sawmills and gristmills. Roads were a key factor in the processing and distribution of the crops, making it possible to cart the crops to a gristmill or a flour mill and then on to eastern markets.

Settlement of the Hamlet of Springfield (Boalsburg)

In 1765, the provincial land office opened, and a large tract of land was acquired in 1766 by Thomas Poultney. He called the tract the Plantation of Harmony. Benjamin Poultney built a log home on the Harmony Plantation tract in 1774. The relationship between Thomas and Benjamin is not known. The settlement immediately west of Harmony Plantation became known as Springfield because of the spring located at the eastern end of Springfield near the present-day Boalsburg Heritage Museum. The spring originates on the north side of Loop Road directly across from the entrance to the present day Springfield Commons housing development. The stream flows behind what is now the First National Bank.

By the time David Boal, Sr. settled near Springfield in 1789, Springfield (Boalsburg) was an established hamlet. Alexander Dunlap, James Watson (from Linden Hall), Jacob Dunlap, and his son, Michael are thought to have had farms near Springfield.

"The Pine Tree"

Sometime prior to 1820, the mail was delivered to a distinctive pine tree atop the hill to the north overlooking Springfield. Simply called "the pine tree," legend has it that it was used as a trading post by the American Indians and as a meeting place by area residents. This pine tree has since become an iconic symbol of the strength and durability of Boalsburg. The "pine tree" was located between Springfield and Oak Hall. Undoubtably, children from Springfield and Oak Hall co-mingled there from time to time.

Settlement of the Hamlet of Oak Hall

The Oak Hall tract traces back to a large piece of property surveyed in the warrantee name of Benjamin Bayless with letters of patent granted to Samuel Wallis. In 1768 Wallis deeded the land to Reuben Haines, who in turn, about 1800, sold it to George McCormick, Sr. George McCormick, Sr. is possibly the first settler of Oak Hall, but it is not known if he actually lived in what would later become the village of Oak Hall.

McCormick is known in local history as a miller who was the first settler of Spring Mills before 1800. McCormick's name appears in the Ferguson Township assessments of 1801 (which would have included the Oak Hall vicinity) as owner of a gristmill and a sawmill in Oak Hall. In 1811, McCormick sold a portion of his Oak Hall tract to his son, George McCormick, Jr., and a 132-acre portion to John Irvin, Sr. Two years later, McCormick's son sold his portion to Jacob Hubler.

The Johnstonbaugh House, Oak Hall, PA

In 1820, Jacob Johnstonbaugh purchased Hubler's property at Oak Hall. Johnstonbaugh was married to Hubler's daughter Susannah, and had, as early as 1819, been assessed for a gristmill and a sawmill in the township. He built a homestead beside Spring Creek about halfway between the Irwin mansion and the present-day Hanson Quarry. This house, now called the Johnstonbaugh house, was in close proximity to his gristmill and sawmill. It is not known if Jacob and his wife occupied the Johnstonbaugh House.

Settlement of the Hamlet of Linden Hall

James and Anne Watson owned one of the earliest farms in upper Penns Valley and built their home on Cedar Creek before 1778. Following a reported encounter with American Indians in May 1778, all the settlers in the vicinity of Linden Hall fled to the safety of Lewistown. Today, this exodus is called the "Great Runaway." Settlers began to return to the valley in the mid to late 1780s. It is reported that James and Ann Watson were the first permanent settlers to return to the area that became known as Linden Hall. By 1785, the American Indians had exited Centre County.

John Irwin emigrated to upper Penns Valley in 1794 and built a successful still at the head of Cedar Creek. He set up housekeeping in a log house near his still.

Rock Hill

Rock Hill was a small settlement about ½ mile north of Linden Hall. It no longer exists as a settlement.

Dale's Mills

Christian Dale moved to Centre County in 1790. He began farming about ½ mile north of the present-day village of Oak Hall. Eventually, Christian and his son Felix established a gristmill and a sawmill. Felix established a hemp mill a number of years later. Dale's Mills ceased to exist as a thriving community, probably in the late 1870s. Dale's Mills is now a part of Lemont.

Earlystown

Earlystown was a small settlement consisting of several buildings and a tavern/inn. It is believed that the settlement was located where Earlystown Road (State Route 45) intersects with the old stagecoach road. It was not a successful community, probably because of its close proximity to Linden Hall and the gristmill that was located in Linden Hall. It no longer exists.

Development of Roads

The importance of a network of roads to regional development should not be overlooked. From the early period of settlements, parts of the upper Penns Valley, in particular, Boalsburg, Oak Hall, and Linden Hall have been linked. Parts of northern and western Centre County were also linked to Potter's Mills and subsequently to the eastern seaboard markets.

Probably by 1792, with the opening of the Centre Furnace, the Huntingdon path and a spur likely built from Lewistown to Potters Mills and beyond to Springfield (Boalsburg) would have been widened to accommodate wagon traffic. Businesses began to emerge along Earlystown Road and Boalsburg Pike from Linden Hall to General Benner's Road (now Benner Pike) to cater to the wagon traffic.

Centre Furnace, State College, PA

During this time, toll roads proliferated in America. In the 1790s, the Boalsburg-Potters Mills toll road and Boalsburg Pike were probably built. The stone bridge at the east end of Springfield may have been part of the Springfield-Potter's Mills toll road. With the emergence of iron furnaces along Bald Eagle Creek, Bellefonte (established in 1798) was growing rapidly, leading to an increased demand for consumer goods. There are indications that Boalsburg Pike from Oak Hall to beyond Dale's Mills was also a toll road. There were toll roads from Springfield to Potter's Mills and from Potter's Mills to Lewistown.

Foundation for Growth

After the Revolutionary War, America entered a period of serious economic downturn, termed the Economic Crisis of the 1780s. As the Revolutionary War ended in 1781, the economy was in shambles. Exports to Britain were restricted by the Crown. Thus, a major source of colonial era commerce was eliminated. A flood of cheap British manufactured imports that sold cheaper than comparable American-made goods made the post-war economic slump worse. Finally, the high level of debt taken on by the states to fund the war effort added to the distress. Inflation rose to over 60% by the end of the decade. To exacerbate the situation, states printed their own currency and levied import taxes on goods from other states.

Stone bridge at east end of Springfield

There was a collapse in credit, as ordinary American farmers borrowed heavily to establish farms or homes and were unable to meet repayments due to the slumping agricultural markets. Creditors saw their wealth evaporate.

America may have emerged from the Revolutionary War victorious, but economically it was in dire straits. Both the new national government and the states were left with massive war debts. There was a shortage of hard currency. American governments had attempted to fund the war through excessive printing of paper money. By 1781, a paper Continental dollar was worth about five per cent of a silver dollar. The country and its states were bankrupt and in considerable debt. It is little wonder that very little in the way of growth, especially on the frontier, occurred.

In 1888, the Constitution of the Unite States was ratified. The Constitution created a new federal government with unpresented powers. There was a feeling of confidence among the citizens.

The decade of the 1790s were a period of economic recovery. In 1792, Centre Furnace became the first major business to open in Centre County. In 1797, the Milesburg Iron Works opened. In, Boalsburg, a few stores began to open.

BIRTH OF EASTERN CENTRE COUNTY INDUSTRY, 1800-1819

Some notable local events occurring from the 1800 to 1819 that signify early growth are:

Circa 1800—Christian and Felix Dale build a gristmill and sawmill at what would become known as Dale's Mills

Circa 1801—George McCormick builds a gristmill and sawmill at what would become known as Oak Hall

1802—The first Rock Hill School is built at Linden Hall

1804—David Boal, Jr. opens the Boal Tavern/inn in Springfield

Circa 1804—Stagecoach begins local operation connecting Springfield to Lewisburg

1808—John Irvin builds a gristmill in Linden Hall

1810—John Irwin completes building a brick home in Linden Hall

1810—Andrew Stroup lays out a plan for the village of Springfield

1810—The first schoolhouse in Springfield is built

1810—Curtin Iron Works near Bellefonte opens

Circa 1815—Cross-state travel via stagecoach is established

Circa 1815—A schoolhouse is built in upper Oak Hall

Circa 1818—Cottage industries emerge

1819—Boalsburg Tavern is built

The period of time between 1800 and 1819 was a period of transition. As the region transitioned from producing whiskey to producing dry grain products like flour and feed, there was an increase in local wagon traffic. With these changes came demands for better roads and services. Soon it may have been possible for one to travel from the Benner Road to Lewistown almost entirely on toll roads.

During this 20-year transition period, small businesses began to emerge and commerce began to accelerate, even though money was tight. Bellefonte began to grow at a rapid pace, too, bringing with it all the demands for eastern consumer goods. Many of these goods would likely have passed via wagon through Springfield and Oak Hall. Outside monies began to flow into the region. Cottage industries began to develop signaling the birth of American industry.. Generally speaking, population growth and industrial growth occur concurrently. One can often access population growth by examining the growth of schools, churches, and post offices.

Schools

The earliest school built in the upper Penns Valley was the one built at Rock Hill in 1802. The original Rock Hill school was a log structure, and heat was provided by a large stone fireplace. The school was for boys only. The first teacher at Rock Hill school was William Smith, Sr.

The first schoolhouse in Springfield was built in 1810 about the time the town was first laid out by Andrew Stroup. It was thought to have been just east of the present Harris Township office building on the corner of Loop Road and Pitt (Main) St. The first teacher was Captain Thomas Evans.

Around 1815, a schoolhouse was built in Oak Hall. It was called the upper schoolhouse, as a second schoolhouse would be built later.

Upper schoolhouse in Oak Hall, ca. 1810, Oak Hall, PA

Other early schools in the area were Walnut Grove (located near the entrance to Bear Meadows Road), Branch School (between Boalsburg and State College), and Shingletown School. The dates when these schools were built are unknown. The Walnut Grove school was used until 1921 when the building was sold.

Pre-War-of-1812 Growth

At the turn of the century, farming was the principle occupation in rural America. As the population grew, settlers congregated along well-travelled roads. Sawmills and gristmills were the first businesses to appear. Streams were important to where these businesses were located, as early mills were powered by water. Hamlets began to evolve into villages as small businesses emerged. In the early formative years of America, the primary non-farming economic activity involved sending raw materials to be used by cities along the eastern seaboard or to be shipped abroad to producers of finished products in Europe. Among the primary exports were charcoal iron and logs. Charcoal iron was produced by numerous small furnaces located throughout Centre County, especially along Bald Eagle Creek and elsewhere. Centre Furnace began operation in 1792. The Curtin Iron Works near Bellefonte began operation in 1810.

Increased Wagon Traffic and the Stagecoach

During this early transition period, the population of the three hamlets grew into villages. A contributing factor aside from increased wagon traffic was the establishment of the stagecoach, which stimulated an increase in the number of artisans and craftsmen starting small businesses to service and repair wagons or to sell finished products to through travelers.

The first stagecoach route through Centre County was from Lewisburg, through Aaronsburg, Millheim, Spring Mills, Springfield, Pine Grove Mills, and on to Spruce Creek. A route from Philadelphia to Spruce Creek, through Springfield would later follow.

Thus, Springfield became an important hub for local and cross-state stagecoach travelers. The local stagecoach came first. The beginning of local service probably coincided closely with the opening of the Boal Tavern in Springfield in 1804.

The local stagecoach road leaving Linden Hall passed in front of the John Irwin House, forded Cedar Creek and joined Earlystown Road about a mile away. At this junction was a hamlet called Earlystown. There stood an inn/tavern and several other buildings. The tavern was one of the earliest establishments in the county along the stage route. It was first recorded on the County tax list in 1808. It was built after the Boal Tavern and was demolished in the 1920s.

The cross-state Philadelphia-Pittsburgh stagecoach route was built piecemeal and likely came around 1812-15.

In 1810, Andrew Stroup developed a site plan for the village of Springfield. He sold ¼ acre lots for $11 and more. This was a sign of the early growth of Springfield. David Boal, Jr. later laid out an addition of the western end of the village in 1832. By 1811, there were two houses, a tavern, and a tannery located in the eastern end of the village. More were to soon follow. It would appear that the eastern end of town may have developed more slowly than the western end of town. Few homes seem to have been built east of Morris (Academy) Street until after 1835. This may have been because no one wanted to live near the tannery and its foul odor.

With the growth of wagon traffic and the beginning of stagecoach service there became an increase demand for craftsmen, artisans, and other small businesses to perform wagon services and repairs. Other craftsmen sold various consumer goods to through travelers.

Craftsmen, Artisans. and Small Businesses

The establishment of businesses and road improvements led to increased wagon traffic through the three villages. More wagon traffic justified the establishment of businesses that catered specifically to the needs of the waggoneers. These businesses were scattered throughout Oak Hall, Linden Hall, and Springfield by 1804, signifying the growth of the region and Centre County. Waggoneers and travelers on dusty roads needed a watering hole. So, the Boal Tavern was established in Springfield (Boalsburg) in 1804. The tavern had room for overnight travelers.

Early businesses can be conveniently categorized into three groups. The first group of businesses grew up around farming. These businesses were **gristmills** and **sawmills**. The first settlers in Penns Valley would have had to take their grain to mills in Lewisburg or Sunbury, which involved a trip of several days' duration. As the area became more settled, local gristmills began to spring up along streams in upper Penns Valley to serve the growing number of farming families.

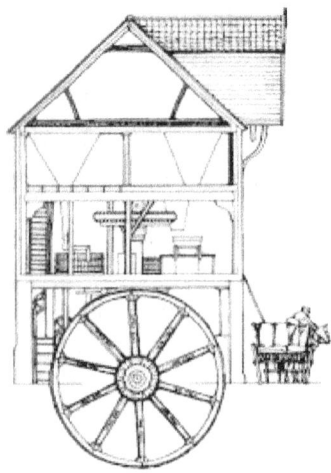

Typical configuration of an early Colonial gristmill

The earliest gristmill in upper Penns Valley was built by Christian and Felix Dale along Spring Creek in Dale's Mills around the turn of the 19th century. The Dale's Mills gristmill was conveniently located on Boalsburg Pike so it could readily accommodate local farmers and farmers from the northern and western part of Centre County. This mill proved to be very successful and by 1805, the Dales were wealthy.

In 1801, George McCormick, Sr. built a gristmill in Oak Hall. In 1808, John Irvin, Sr. built a gristmill in Linden Hall on Cedar Creek. John Irwin later built a mill pond to provide an adequate and continuous supply of water. The mill was later destroyed by fire. The mill in Linden Hall would appear to have catered primarily to local farmers. But nevertheless, it was successful.

The second group of businesses catered to waggoneers to service and repair wagons. Among these were tanners, blacksmiths, and carriage shops.

Typical configuration of an early Colonial tannery (McElhoe 2015)

The only known **tannery** in the area was the one operated in Springfield. The tannery was located at the eastern end of the village. It began operations about the same time as the Boal Tavern in 1804.

The original operator of the tannery in Springfield was William Murray followed by Jonathan Mosser in 1837. Mr. Mosser owned considerable mountain land from which he gathered timber for the tanning process. He got water from a nearby spring via wooden pipes. Water was discharged into four 10' X 10' X 8' vats. After the animal hide was scraped and cleaned, it was put into a solution of ground bark. Oak bark made white leather, and hemlock bark made red leather. The power to grind the bark was supplied by a white horse named Charlie. Mr. Mosser hitched Charlie to a long arm that turned a grinding mill as Charlie walked in a circle.

Blacksmith shoeing a horse (McElhoe 2015)

Blacksmith shops opened during the early years of Springfield. Among the early shops was one was located near the eastern end of Pitt Street and a second was located on Morris Street next to Mr. J. Logue's carriage shop on Morris (Academy) Street. Both were operated by Mr. Logue.

Blacksmiths were among the earliest craftsmen operating in Oak Hall and Linden Hall. They were in high demand. There were at least two blacksmith shops in and around Oak Hall and at least two in and around Linden Hall.

The skilled craftsman in a **carriage shop** was the wheelwright. Various names are associated with wheelwrights, such as wagonmaker, cartwright, and coachmaker. In Colonial times, almost

55

A wheelwright at work (McElhoe 2015)

everything a man could not carry on his back or on a horse was moved on wheels via wagons. Therefore, wheelwrights were sorely needed. A carriage shop was closely associated with blacksmithing, and carriage shops were often located near blacksmith shops. The first carriage shop in Springfield was opened by James Loupe and was located at the eastern end of town on Morrison (Academy) Street. Soon thereafter, several other carriage shops opened.

It seems logical that the third group of businesses to evolve were those catering to stagecoach travelers. The principal early business catering to travelers was the tavern. Here travelers could get food and drink. An added plus was the luxury of overnight accommodations. While all locales in the area had taverns, only Springfield and Linden Hall are thought to have offered overnight accommodations. The Boal Tavern opened in 1804. In 1819, the Boalsburg Tavern opened. The tavern/inn at L:inden Hall (Earlystown) probably opened in 1808. All three accommodated travelers and had barns for the horses. Springfield became a routine overnight stop for stagecoach travelers.

In 1819, Col. James Johnson completed building the Boalsburg Tavern on the diamond in Boalsburg. The original building was a five-bay, center hall, Georgian style structure. The Boalsburg Tavern was built to serve the "gentry." Drovers were not welcome as overnight guests.

Other Small Businesses

Probably after the stagecoach began operating, a number of small businesses emerged that would have catered to travelers from out-of-town. The items offered were more in the category of "luxury" items of the day. The artisans were a seamstress, boot makers, a gunsmith, a tinsmith, a tanner, and more. Boalsburg was largely

The Boalsburg Tavern, circa 1910, Boalsburg (Horner 2019)

the center of these activities, although Linden Hall did have a boot maker. To serve farmers came coopers and cradle makers.

Post-War-of-1812 Growth

After the war of 1812, with the encouragement of the federal government, entrepreneurs in America began producing finished products for American consumers instead of relying on European producers. Thus, American industry was born.

In its infancy, the first industries in the three-village region were likely cottage industries. The first reported cottage industry in the region was the production of flax. Around circa 1818, the flax cottage industry began to emerge in the region, particularly in Boalsburg. Flax plants were grown locally and then spun into fibers.

The fibers of the flax plant were used for rope, twine, matting, cloth, and numerous other uses. Producing flax was very labor intensive and gradually, with the growth of slavery in the south and the widespread use of the cotton gin, cotton replaced flax for many uses.

Emergence of Viable Villages

There were two primary reasons why the Boalsburg-Oak Hall-Linden Hall region developed into a thriving center of growth.

The first factor that led to growth was the Whiskey Rebellion which probably caused farmers to begin to produce solid grain products in lieu of whiskey. Unfortunately, farmers had to take their grain to distant locations (at least two days travel) to be ground into usable products. It follows that the next logical development was the building of gristmills in the immediate area. Exiting eastern Centre County at Potter's Mills was now a viable exit point. The above two factors made this possible.

The three village s were well suited to take advantage of the opening of the Potter's Mills exit. First, they were located at the confluence of multiple well-traveled and still developing roadways. By traveling through the area, travelers could avoid crossing Nittany Mountain. Also, as the area began to develop, it was a conveniently located place to get food and drink, overnight accommodations, and wagon repairs.

By 1804, the local stagecoach was probably operating.

The area rapidly became a gateway to eastern markets. After the War of 1812, with the encouragement of the federal government, Americans began producing products for local consumption. Cottage industries began to emerge.

The growth of small-scale artisan businesses like a tannery, blacksmiths, sawmills, gristmills, and flax milling show a growing sense of economic development. Further, the opening af a new school is a sign of economic growth.

Cottage Industry

THE PROSPEROUS YEARS, 1820-1855

There were numerous signs of the growth and prosperity of the Boalsburg-Oak Hall-Linden Hall community. Among the significant local events are:

1820—A new post office is established in Boalsburg

Circa 1820—The "Lewis and Connelly Gang" eliminated as a menace to travelers passing through Seven Mountians

Circa 1820-1830—Numerous mills open for business in Oak Hall/Dale's Mills area

1822—The James Irwin brick mill in Oak Hall is built

1825—James Irwin completes building the Irwin mansion in Oak Hall

1827—The construction of Zion Union Church (The Old Stone Church) brings two new churches from Oak Hall to Boalsburg

1830—The first Rock Hill/Linden Hall school burns down

1835—Harris Township is established

1837—The panic of 1837 begins

1840—The second Rock Hill/Linden Hall school is built

1853—Boalsburg Academy opens

1855—The Farmers' High School, now known as The Pennsylvania State University, opens

Circa 1855—Stagecoach ceases to operate

There were also ominous signs heralding the negative effects of the Industrial Revolution. Some of the major events were:

1834—The opening of the Allegheny Portage Railroad

1854—The opening of the horseshoe curve in Altoona, which made cross-state travel via all rail possible

1855—The closing of the Allegheny Portage Railroad

The 1820 census showed that there were 13,718 persons living in Centre County.

With the "Lewis and Connelly Gang" no longer a menace, plans were made for a turnpike between Lewistown and Bellefonte. If this road passed through Springfield, it would have greatly enhanced the wagon traffic through Boalsburg and Oak Hall. The economic activity during this period was quite different in Linden Hall than it was in Boalsburg and Oak Hall. Oak Hall had mills that produced finished products. Boalsburg had no mills, but supplied much of the labor needed to operate the Oak Hall mills. Accordingly, there would have been ample outside monies flowing into these two villages to support numerous "luxury" artisans, such as hatters, seamstresses, tinsmiths, boot makers, gun smiths, and others. Additionally, there was much outside wagon and stagecoach traffic to support the blacksmiths, tanner, and carriage makers. The economy of Linden Hall seemed to be largely dependent on agriculture. The wagon and stagecoach traffic in Linden Hall would appear to have been largely local.

Several flour mills were built in the Oak Hall-Boalsburg area during this time. A flour mill was built 1 mile east of Boalsburg on Spring Creek. The remnants of this mill can still be seen. But the date this mill was established is not known, except that it was prior to 1860. George McCormick, Sr. built a flour mill in Oak Hall in 1801. There was also a flour mill at Dale's Mills. There were two sawmills in Oak Hall (including the one built by Christian Dale, circa 1800). James Irwin, John's son, also built a brick mill in Oak Hall in 1822. There was also a gristmill and sawmill operating at Millheim.

Post Offices

In 1820, the U.S. Postal Service decided to establish a post office in the Springfield area. At the time, the eastern end of the village was called Springfield, and the western end was called Boalsburg. The western end of town seemed to have developed more rapidly, so when the post office was established in 1820, the postal address of the town became officially known as Boalsburg, by vote of the citizens of the two villages. It is not known if the village was named after David Boal, Sr. or David Boal, Jr. or just the Boal family.

The first Boalsburg postmaster was Col. John Hassen. He was appointed in 1820. At that time, the mail drop location was at the discretion of the Postmaster. Legend has it that the first drop off point was a hollow tree, but this point cannot be confirmed. Later, the mail drop may have been moved to the Boalsburg Tavern. This point cannot be confirmed either. It was next moved to a room in the Sarah Johnson home. Sometime later, the drop off point was moved to a narrow brick building, built in 1835. This building is next door to the Boalsburg Tavern.

In 1847, the U.S. Postmaster General issued the first two U.S. postage stamps bearing the likenesses of George Washington and Benjamin Franklin, the country's first Postmaster General. It cost 5 cents to mail a letter weighing less than 1 oz that was going 300 miles or less. In Boalsburg, it may have been about this time that the postal drop off point was moved to the narrow, two-story brick building next to the Boalsburg Tavern, because a more secure facility was needed rather than a simple drop off point. For 15 years or more, residents of Oak Hall and Linden Hall probably had to venture to Boalsburg to buy stamps.

Schools

In 1830, the Rock Hill/Linden Hall school burned down. A second school was built in 1840.

It has been written by Corter that there was one school in Boalsburg located on the eastern end of Pitt Street. If correct, then sometime prior to 1860, the school was moved to Pine Street east of the old Methodist Church building. The new school building was supposedly a one story, brick structure that was remodeled into a two story, frame structure.

But the people of Boalsburg were desirous that their children be well educated beyond grammar school. Thus, a group of men, Rev. Peter Fisher, George Boal, Henry Keller, and George Jack established the Boalsburg Academy in 1853. The private academy provided a liberal-minded education. The land for the academy was obtained from Col. James Johnson, the same James Johnson who built the Boalsburg Tavern in 1819. The eight weeks of the summer term cost $5.00.

Oak Hall Mills

The development of Boalsburg and Oak Hall was led by the opening of various mills and small businesses that sprang up in the Oak Hall-Dale's Mills area during the decade of the 1820s. There were two woolen mills, a hemp mill, a clover mill, several sawmills, two gristmills, a brick mill, and multiple blacksmith shops. James Irwin built a brick mill in 1822 called the Irwin mill. John Irwin of Linden Hall built many of these mills. These mills employed numerous workers from Boalsburg and the surrounding area.

Typical mode of transportation in the early to mid-1800s

The importance of these mills should not be overlooked. Outside money flowed into Oak Hall, and subsequently, into Boalsburg and Linden Hall in the form of employee wages. Boalsburg and Linden Hall did not develop mills, but instead were content to provide a workforce for the mills in Oak Hall. The John Irwin gristmill was the only mill known to have been built in Linden Hall, possibly due to the comparatively small size of Cedar Creek.

The outside monies, along with the stagecoach and wagon traffic, fueled the growth in the number of craftsmen and artisans in all three villages.

In 1883, Centre County historian John Blair Linn wrote that Oak Hall owed its importance to the energy and enterprise of General James Irvin, son of John Irwin of Linden Hall. James Irvin, who looms large in local history as a prominent ironmaster,

Typical size of mill in the early 1800s

Remnants of the Irwin Mill along Spring Creek, Oak Hall, PA

burg-Oak Hall-Linden Hall area. In addition to the businesses along Spring Creek, the villages supported taverns, carriage shops, blacksmith shops, a tannery, and many small businesses and artisans. Among the artisans were shoemakers, wheelwrights, coopers, hatters, broom makers, tinsmiths, tailors, a carpet maker, and more. The area also supported a limestone quarry, a lime kiln, iron ore pits, iron furnaces, and farms. These businesses provided stable, year-round employment for many area residents. There was a steady influx of outside money flowing into the local community.

Increasing wagon traffic passed down Boalsburg Pike to Boalsburg en route to the eastern seaboard. Boalsburg became a gateway to the east. Boalsburg also became a favored stagecoach stop on one of many routes from Philadelphia to Pittsburgh.

The Coming of the Iron Horse

One of the more significant and early developments of the industrial revolution was the railroad. Railroads in America can be traced back to 1815 when Col. John Stevens gained the first charter in North America for the New Jersey Railroad (NJRR)

The Irwin Mansion, Oak Hall, PA

Company, although the Camden and Amboy Railroad as it was later called was not constructed until 1832. The NJRR later became part of the Pennsylvania Railroad's sprawling network. Col. Stevens is recognized by many as the father of American railroads.

A river-canal-rail system between Philadelphia and Pittsburgh opened in 1834. This system included the Allegheny Portage Railroad, and with its completion, it began to erode stagecoach traffic on all Pennsylvania turnpikes, including the one through Boalsburg. Travelers could journey between Pittsburgh and Philadelphia on the river-canal-rail system in three-and-a-half to four-and-a-half days.

The coming of an all-rail Pennsylvania Railroad route between Philadelphia and Pittsburgh over the horseshoe curve in Altoona in 1854 shredded cross-state travel time to 13 hours and also cut the fare from $9.50 to $8.00. Within a decade, Pennsylvanians could travel to almost any location in the state on rail in a single day.

The coming of the railroad had a profound effect on the Boalsburg-Oak Hall-Linden Hall region. The stagecoach oper-

Allegheny Portage Railroad

ation went out of business around 1855. As the Pennsylvania Railroad expanded into small communities throughout the state, Boalsburg and many other communities became isolated. Wagon traffic down Boalsburg Pike began to diminish as more and more freight was transported via rail.

Railroads isolated many small communities like Boalsburg, Oak Hall, and Linden Hall.

Other Developments

The early development of Oak Hall included three homes. There is the Johnstonbaugh house, the Irwin mansion, and the Foster house. Each displays a unique character highlighting the skills of the craftsmen of early America.

The Foster house is possibly the oldest in Oak Hall. This stone farmhouse located at the beginning of Linden Hall Road in Oak Hall was built in 1820 and possibly first owned by the Hastings family. Afterwards, it changed hands many times until 1870 when the Holman family bought it and upgraded it to a Victorian-style home. They kept the farm for close to 100 years until it was sold to the Smiths, who spent the next 10 years restoring the burnt structure.

In 1835, Harris Township was established. Harris Township was formed from parts of Ferguson and several other townships. It was named after James Harris, who was a founder of Bellefonte in 1798, as well as its first postmaster and its first state senator. In 1836, there were about 270 persons on the tax roll.

The Foster House, Oak Hall, PA

The Panic of 1837

The Panic of 1837 was a financial crisis in the United States that touched off a major recession that lasted until circa 1848. Profits, prices, and wages went down while unemployment went up. Pessimism abounded during the time. During the "Panic," banks collapsed, businesses failed, prices declined, and thousands of workers lost their jobs. Unemployment may have been as high as 25% in some locales. The years 1837 to 1844 were, generally speaking, years of deflation in wages and prices.

Those producing pig iron and operating furnaces were hit particularly hard. The price received per ton for pig iron declined by about 40% or more. In Pennsylvania more than half of the furnaces failed. Also, a third of the forges and 18% of its rolling mills failed. In Centre County, five of the nine ironworks failed.

There were many causes. Among them were new, cost-efficient technologies used by English iron producing competitors and a reduction in American tariff rates. Tariff rates were fiercely debated in the U.S. Congress for about 40 years. The consequent "Panic" and the coming of the railroad were harbingers of a difficult future to come that would plague the region for years. The Panic of 1837 signified the end of an extended period of prosperity of the region.

The Coming of Penn State

The promotion of agriculture and the sharing of information was the impetus for the call by the Agricultural Society of Pennsylvania for a new Farmers' High School.

In 1855, James Irvin of Oak Hall and Moses Thompson offered 200-250 acres of Centre Furnace land to establish the Farmers' High School, the forerunner of The Pennsylvania State University. The Commonwealth of Pennsylvania chartered the school as one of the nation's first colleges of agricultural sciences with a goal to apply scientific principles to farming.

Farmers' High School, circa 1860, State College, PA

Rise and Decline of Prosperity

Two factors were major contributors to the growth and economic prosperity of the region. Both factors brought in outside monies to support growth. Indicators of growth were that the area was able to support many artisans and craftsmen.

The first factor was the mills in Oak Hall. Most early mills relied on water power, and Oak Hall and Dale's Mills were well positioned along Spring Creek to take advantage of this power source. Boalsburg and Linden Hall provided much of the labor to operate these mills. As products were sold, outside monies came into Oak Hall and Dale's Mills. Through employee wages, some of this income made its way to the surrounding area. It eventually supported small businesses.

The second factor was the presence of the stagecoach, which brought travelers to the area. These travelers probably were frequent visitors to the small businesses in the area, thus further stimulating economic growth. Food and drink and the availability of overnight accommodations further added to the attractiveness of the region as a favored stagecoach stop. Two factors would lead to the end of the period of prosperity. The first was the "Panic of 1837." The Panic touched off a major recession in the country that lasted until circa 1848. Banks failed, prices rose, wages went down, and many lost their jobs. One of the possible consequences of the Panic may have been a decline in regional population.

The second factor leading to the decline in prosperity was the coming of the Pennsylvania Railroad. Cross state travel via the railroad rapidly replaced cross state travel via stagecoach. The stagecoach likely went out of business shortly after the horseshoe curve in Altoona was completed in 1854. The closing of the stagecoach was a major economic loss to the area.

Points of Interest

Listed on the following page are points of interest listed on the 1861 map of Centre County by Tilden. These points of interest may have been functional enterprises as late as 1860.

The 1861 map is not sufficiently detailed to show points of interest in the three villages. The portion of the map studied does not include Shingletown, Lemont, Centre Hall, or Old Fort. (see map on page 11 in Appendix A.)

Type	Point of Interest	Location	Est.	Comments
School	School No. 1	Rock Hill	1802	Probably the first Rock Hill School
Church	Unnamed church No. 1	½ mi. north of Lin-den Hall in Rock Hill		
General store	Store—D. Hess & P. Meyer	Linden Hall		
Mill	Flour mill—J. Meyer	Linden Hall	1808	This mill was built by John Irvin
Business	Blacksmith shop—J. Meyer	Linden Hall		
Business	Blacksmith shop	1 mi. west of Linden Hall		
Business	Woolen Mill—J. G Irvin	Oak Hall		
School	Unnamed school	Oak Hall		Called the Upper Oak Hall School
Business	Flour mill	Oak Hall	1823	The Irwin mill
Business	Foundry	Oak Hall		
Business	Saw mill	Oak Hall		
Business	Toll House	north of Oak Hall		On Earlystown Road
Church	Unnamed church	Oak Hall		Believed to be the Albright Church
Business	Store—H. S. Faber	Oak Hall		
Business	Saw mill	Dale's Mills		
Business	Dale store	Dale's Mills		
Business	Tannery	Boalsburg		
Business	Flour mill—S. Wilson	1 mi. east of Boalsburg		
School	Unnamed school	2 mi. east of Boalsburg		Believed to be the Walnut Grove School

71

TRANSITION FROM WAGONS TO MOTORIZED TRAVEL, 1856-1913

Centre Furnace ceased operations in 1858. Oil was discovered in NW Pennsylvania in 1859. Additionally, the Pennsylvania logging industry was at the beginning of a state of decline, as many ridges had been stripped bare of trees with no plan for reforestation. The easy timber had been harvested by circa 1880. The PA logging industry was essentially all gone by the 1920s. Residents of rural communities like the Boalsburg-Oak Hall-Linden Hall area began to migrate to the cities, industrial centers, and oil fields in search of jobs. The rural population of Pennsylvania began to decline. The three-village economy, which was based on wagon traffic and stagecoach operations, was ill prepared when the stagecoach ceased operating and as America transitioned to motorized travel.

Some of the more notable local events are:
1858—The Centre Furnace closes for business
1860—The Egg Hill Evangelical Brethren Church is built on Egg Hill
1862—St. John's German Reformed Church builds a new church in Boalsburg
1862—A mail drop is established in Linden Hall
1868—The Old Stone Church in Boalsburg is demolished, making way for the Zion Lutheran Church
1868—The St. John's German Reformed Church installs the first pipe organ in Centre County

1879—The lower schoolhouse in Oak Hall is built
1885—The L&T Railroad comes to Linden Hall and Oak Hall
Circa 1885—Whitmer and Reitz Company begins logging in Bear Meadows
1885—Huyett and Livingood begins producing rail cars
Circa 1890—McCoy and Linn begin producing charcoal for local iron furnaces
1886—A mail drop is established on the hill near the "pine tree" between Oak Hall and Boalsburg
1892—The Boalsburg Fire Company is organized
1893—Boalsburg Academy closes
1893—The second Rock Hill/Linden Hall school was demolished and replaced with the third Rock Hill/Linden Hall school
1895—Linden Hall Lumber Company moves to Linden Hall, sets up a sawmill in the village beside Cedar Run, and begins producing lumber
1897—The Boalsburg Water Company is established
1897—Evangelical Methodist Church is built in Linden Hall
1905—Most timber-related operations leave Linden Hall because there was no more timber

Churches

In 1860, the German Reformed Church in Boalsburg sold its interest in the Old Stone Church to the Lutheran Congregation for $3.50 and began planning for a church building of its own. In 1862, the German Reformed Congregation dedicated their new church on Miller Street (now Church Street). This was the third church building built in Boalsburg.

In 1868, St. John's German Reformed Church installed a pipe organ built by Charles F. Dürner of Quakertown, PA. It was the first pipe organ in Centre County. Joseph Meyer of Boalsburg, was largely responsible for the procurement and payment for the cost of the organ. Joseph Meyer died while playing the organ the day before the organ was dedicated.

That same year (1868), the Zion Union Church (Old Stone Church) was demolished due to structural deficiencies in favor of a new

Zion Lutheran Church, which was built on the same site.

At one time there were four church congregations in Boalsburg. In addition to the two churches mentioned above, a Methodist Church was established in 1833. The Church building was located on Pine Street, just west of the school building. It is not known when the building was demolished. Unfortunately, this congregation was small and did not survive. They may have become inactive around 1870.

The German Reformed Church, ca. 1862, Boalsburg, PA

There was also a Presbyterian Church that shared the building with the Boalsburg Academy on Morris (Academy) Street. There is very little known about this Congregation. There are no references to this church in any writings after the 1900 time frame.

The original Evangelical Church in Linden Hall was the first church built in Linden Hall. The exact date that this church was built is unknown. The Evangelical Congregation in Linden Hall was divided into two loosely arranged groups, the Esherites and the Dubsites. In the early 1880s, a dispute arose between the two groups, causing the Dubsites to leave the church. The Esherites continued to use the original building for worship, but by the early 1900s the Esherite Congregation became inactive. Over the next 25-30 years, the building deteriorated. It was disassembled in 1933.

The Dubsites purchased a tract of land on the corner of the John T. Ross lane. There, in 1897, they built a new church across Ross Lane from the original building. Today, the church is known as the Evangelical Methodist Church. It was the second church built in Linden Hall and is still standing. There is no written record of another church being built in Linden Hall. The Evangelical Methodist Church was built during the height of the economic resurgence from the logging and lumber operations.

In 1902, the St. John's German Reformed Church underwent a $7,000 remodeling project.

Post Offices

In 1862, a mail drop was established in Linden Hall. The mail drop was located in the store operated by Daniel Hess. It was not known if postage stamps were sold at this mail drop. In 1886, a mail drop was established in Oak Hall. Residents of Oak Hall and possibly Linden Hall have had to travel to Boalsburg to purchase stamps.

Schools

Circa 1855, the Boalsburg school was moved to a building on Pine Street. The original building on Pine Street was a one-story brick structure. It was later replaced by a two-story wood frame structure. The date of this upgrade is not known.

The Harris Township School Board had many financial woes in the late 1800s and early 1900s. It was a common practice for individuals to make short-term loans to the school board.

The school on Pine Street, ca. 1910, Boalsburg, PA

The teacher of the Boalsburg Academy in 1862 was James Patterson. When President Lincoln called for more soldiers to fight in the Civil War, Mr. Patterson met with his students in the Old Stone Church and organized Company G of the 148th Pennsylvania Volunteers. Most of Mr. Patterson's class joined Company G and went to war. The Academy was closed during the Civil War.

A new one-room schoolhouse was built in Oak Hall in 1879 across from the Irwin mansion to replace the upper schoolhouse. It was referred to as the lower schoolhouse.

The Lower School House, Oak Hall, PA

The Boalsburg Academy was permanently closed in the 1880s. At the time it was closed, the area occupied by the Academy was taken over by the Harris Township School Board who used it as a high school. The building was deemed unsafe. The building and lot were purchased by the Presbyterians in 1892. They demolished the original structure and built a new house of worship in 1892.

The last class at the Academy had only 24 students. The closing of the Academy was possibly a sign of the declining population in the region. This second structure still stands on Morris (Academy) Street.

The third Rock Hill/Linden Hall School

A third one-room Rock Hill schoolhouse was built in Linden Hall (Rock Hill) in 1893. The Rock Hill school was built in the same location as the second Rock Hill school.

The Civil War Era

In 1861, southern states began to secede from the Union. Fort Sumter in Charleston Harbor was bombarded, and the Civil War began. Company G of the 148th Pennsylvania Volunteers was formed in the Old Stone Church in 1862. Young men from throughout the region, including Boalsburg, Oak Hall, Linden Hall, and the surrounding area, joined to fight for the Union cause. In 1865, the Confederate states surrendered, and the period called Reconstruction began.

In addition to the absence of those who served, the Civil War had an indirect but profound effect on Oak Hall and the surrounding region. The Civil War created a demand for large amounts of war materials. The factories built in New England during this period were large, industrialized (driven by steam) facilities that were built to save on labor costs and built for mass production. The small mills built in Oak Hall along Spring Creek likely had difficulty in providing the quantity of material demanded. They may have lost lucrative contracts for this reason. An added advantage of many of

Typical New England factory of the last half of the 19th century

these large, New England factories was that the volume of product could justify a rail line. Many of the mills along Spring Creek went out of business by 1875. Gristmills suffered as well. In 1861, there were four gristmills/flour mills in and around Boalsburg-Oak Hall-Linden Hall. By 1874, there were only two.

The economy of Boalsburg-Oak Hall-Linden Hall, which had been reliant on the mills producing products and transporting these products to eastern markets via wagon, was gone. The growth of American industry caused many mom-and-pop industries throughout America and around the region to close. The era of long-distance wagon travel was beginning to decline.

Decoration Day

The Civil War battle of Gettysburg is thought to have had a considerable impact on the three-village region. In total, 55 young men from Boalsburg who fought in the Civil War are buried in the Boalsburg cemetery. Those killed in action were a significant loss for communities the size of Boalsburg, Oak Hall, and Linden Hall.

One of the soldiers who died was Dr. Reuben Hunter from Boalsburg. Dr. Hunter was an assistant surgeon. He died in September 1864 from typhoid fever. In October 1864, several ladies from Boalsburg gathered at the Boalsburg Cemetery to decorate

The First Memorial Day statue, Boalsburg, PA

the grave of Dr. Hunter. One of the ladies was Emma Hunter, Reuben's daughter. Accompanying her were Sophie Keller and Elizabeth Meyer. There is some disagreement in the written accounts of this event. Some writings say there were three participants; other accounts say there were two. While decorating Dr. Hunter's grave, it was suggested that it would be appropriate to decorate the graves of every soldier buried there, particularly members of the 148th Pennsylvania Volunteers, of which there were many. Thus, the tradition of decorating the graves of soldiers began.

During the first few years, decorating the graves became an annual tradition that seemed to occur each July 4. The celebration in the early years was more like a prayer meeting than a patriotic service. Eventually, the march to the cemetery became a community event, a practice that continues today. First came the drum corps, with Jonathan Cramer playing the fife (small flute). Next came the women and girls carrying flowers, and finally the line of returned soldiers.

On May 8, 1868 General John A. Logan of the Grand Army of the Republic issued a proclamation to honor those who died "in defense of their country during the late rebellion" by decorating the soldier's graves. Known to some as "Decoration Day," mourners honored the Civil War dead by decorating their graves with flowers.

On the first Decoration Day, May 30, 1868, General James Garfield made a speech at Arlington National Cemetery, after which 5,000 participants helped to decorate the graves of the more than 20,000 Civil War soldiers who were buried in the cemetery. The first organized celebration of Decoration Day in Boalsburg occurred on May 30,1869.

After WWI, the federal government declared the last Monday in May to be called Memorial Day as a day to honor all Americans who have died in military service for the United States.

Reconstruction

The Union victory in the Civil War in 1865 may have given some four million slaves their freedom, but the process of rebuilding the South during the Reconstruction period (1865-1876) introduced significant challenges. During the administration of President Andrew Johnson in 1865 and 1866, many southern state legislatures passed restrictive "black codes" to control the labor and behavior of African Americans. Outrage in the North over these codes eroded support for the approach known as Presidential Reconstruction and led to the triumph of a more radical wing of the Republican Party. During Radical Reconstruction, which began in 1867, newly enfranchised blacks gained a voice in government for the first time in American history, winning election to southern state legislatures and even to the U.S. Congress. In less than a decade, however, reactionary forces, such as the Ku Klux Klan, reversed the advances made during Radical Reconstruction in a violent backlash that restored white supremacy to much of the South. Reconstruction was a very violent time in the nation's history, especially in the border states of Missouri and Kentucky. It is generally recognized by historians to have ended in failure in the mid 1870s.

The violence was mainly limited to the South and to the border states, although a few local KKK organizations emerged in southern Pennsylvania. The Boalsburg-Oak Hall-Linden Hall region seemed to escape the violence.

The Industrial Revolution

After the war, factories grew even bigger and more industrialized. Beginning in the mid 1800s, the industrial revolution began in earnest. The industrial revolution had its greatest impact on the lives of most ordinary people and many communities in the country. The industrial revolution had big impacts in the areas of transportation and industry.

Probably the first major development of the industrial revolution was in transportation via the railroad. By the start of the Civil War, railroads had already linked the most important Midwestern cities with the Atlantic coast. With the construction of the transcon-

Typical factory of the last half of the 19th century

tinental railroad in 1869 and the standardization of rail gauges in the 1880s, the railroad quickly became the dominant form of transit for both people and freight.

The Pennsylvania Railroad was formed in 1847. By 1854, the horseshoe curve was completed, and an all-rail link between Philadelphia and Pittsburgh was established. This link significantly reduced cross-state travel time and fares. As a result, the Allegheny Portage Railroad and the stagecoach ceased operation in 1855.

As the nation expanded, so too did the railroads. By 1916, there would be more than 230,000 miles of rail in the United States, and passenger traffic would continue to grow until the end of World War II, when the car and the airplane began to dominate.

With the closures of the stagecoach business and Centre Furnace, most mills along Spring Creek, the decline of the logging industry, and the coming of the railroad, there was a devastating effect on the Boalsburg-Oak Hall-Linden Hall communities, as there was little in the way of outside money coming into the local economy. The Boalsburg-Oak Hall-Linden Hall area became largely isolated, as were many other small villages and towns throughout America. The population began a slow but steady decline as fami-

Model T Ford

lies began migrating to industrial centers and the oil fields of NW Pennsylvania in search of work.

The Industrial Revolution transformed the nation during the late 19th and early 20th centuries. The technological advancements positioned the nation for its rise as a global superpower. An example of an industrial development allowing mass production was the Bessemer process for making steel. The Bessemer process was the first inexpensive industrial process for the mass production of steel from molten pig iron. It was patented in 1856. By the early 1870s, the Bessemer process was being widely used to make steel in industrial centers like Pittsburgh, which greatly increased the demand for pig iron. The small furnaces in the area could not supply the increased demand. Many other industries also began mass production around this time frame.

Motorized Travel

Motorized cars were first developed in the mid 1880s. After the turn of the century, Henry Ford's assembly line processes made automobiles affordable to a large portion of the population. It seems everyone wanted a Model T, or Tin Lizzie. Ford produced the Model T from 1908 through 1927.

The railroad had a huge impact on America

Many cars of that era were open (roadsters), and if you wanted a roof, you had to have one custom made. Some carriage shops in the area began shifting from making wagons and carriages to customizing automobiles. Others simply closed.

Wagon traffic down Boalsburg Pike continued to dwindle. Gottlieb Daimler developed what he called Vehicle no. 42 in 1896. This automobile provided the first truck concept as a horseless wagon with a 4-hp, 2-cylinder engine. Vehicle no. 42 was advertised to pull 3,300 pounds. Mack Trucks, Inc. was founded in 1900

Vehicle no. 42 revolutionnized farming practices

83

The railroad station at Oak Hall, PA

The railroad station at Linden Hall, PA

in Brooklyn, New York by Jack and Gus Mack. It was originally known as the Mack Brothers Company. The British government purchased and employed the Mack AC model to transport food and equipment to its troops during World War I. The extensive use of standardized parts all but eliminated the need for blacksmiths. Truck traffic on Boalsburg Pike began to replace wagon traffic.

L&T Railroad
After much lobbying, mainly by Daniel Hess of Linden Hall, the railroad came to the upper Penns Valley. The Lewisburg and Tyrone (L&T) Railroad finally completed the missing link between Spring Mills and Lemont in 1885. Ironically, the railroad never went to Tyrone. Instead, it was decided that a more profitable route was for the railroad to go around Mt. Nittany, through Linden Hall, Oak Hall, and Lemont, and on to Bellefonte. Travelers could now ride the train from Lewisburg to Bellefonte. From Bellefonte it continued on to Milesburg, Altoona, and beyond. Disaster struck in 1972 when Hurricane Agnes washed out the tracks. The train service was discontinued.

After additional lobbying, train stations were erected in Linden Hall and Oak Hall. The land for the train station in Linden Hall was given by Daniel Hess. By 1886, the Linden Hall and Oak Hall stations were regular stops. Passenger service was discontinued in the late 1930s.

Timbering
The railroad through Linden Hall attracted other businesses. In the mid 1880s, the Whitmer and Reitz Company began cutting timber in the Bear Meadows area. A method called "wildcatting" was used to transport the timber to the rail head in Linden Hall. Flat cars coasted down the mountain over a narrow gauge rail line and came to rest in Linden Hall. Linden Hall was probably selected as the collection point because it provided convenient access to the railroad.

A typical mountaintop scene showing deforestation

The timbering operation spawned to other businesses in Linden Hall, which led a brief period of prosperity for the village. The Linden Hall Lumber Company was chartered in 1885. The company eventually moved its sawmill operations from the Laurel Run area where the timber was being harvested to Linden Hall, near a rail siding of the L&T Railroad (circa 1895).

In 1885, Huyett and Livingood, from Berks and Lebanon Counties, set up a lumber mill in Linden Hall. Their specialty was making wooden railroad cars. Another business that relied on the timbering and lumbering operations was McCoy and Linn, who made charcoal, which they sold to local iron furnaces.

Linden Hall was a very busy timbering location for the last 15 or so years of the 19th century. The activity led to numerous successful general stores and other businesses. Many men were employed on a year-round basis. But at last, the ridges and mountains were bare of timber. In 1905, the bigger timbering operations moved elsewhere. Soon all timbering businesses and all other businesses that had relied on timbering were gone. With the closing of the timber-related businesses the cycle was complete. Linden Hall returned to being a simple farming community.

Leisure Living

The first band in Boalsburg, the Boal Band, was organized before the Civil War. At its height, there were 24 members. Their uniforms were grey with black facings. They had brass buttons. Each band member had an instrument, purchased by the Boal family. The band was awarded prizes in public contests; one location was likely Bellefonte.

The Cornet Band was organized in Linden Hall around 1880. They played at church socials, grange picnics, Memorial Day celebrations, and musical conventions. Competition with the Boal Band was intense.

In the early 1880s, baseball was a favorite past time, and local villages, including Linden Hall, Centre Hall, Spring Mills, and Boalsburg, had baseball teams. Rivalry was fierce among team members and fans, and it was not unusual for fights to break out during games. Sometimes team members were selected for their ability to defend themselves nearly as much as for their baseball skills.

Linden Hall baseball team

Other Regional Developments

Of the various fraternal organizations, the oldest in Boalsburg was the I.O.O.F. No. 894. It was organized in 1874. In 1903, the Maccabees were organized. In 1910, the Knights of Malta were organized. The Woman's Civic Club was another active organization. The Woman's Civic Club of Boalsburg was organized in 1911. Among their notable activities, the Woman's Club assumed a debt of $117.93 for the street lamps in the village. Additionally, they held festivals on the evening of Decoration Day.

The 28th infantry division is a unit of the Army National Guard and is the oldest division-sized unit in the armed forces of the United States. Some of the units of the division can trace their lineage to Benjamin Franklin's battalion, The Pennsylvania Associators (1747-1777). The division was officially established in 1879 and was later designated as the 28th Division in 1917, after the entry of America into the First World War. It is today part of the Pennsylvania Army National Guard, Maryland Army National Guard, Ohio Army National Guard, and New Jersey Army National Guard. Many area residents have served in the 28th.

The Division was originally nicknamed the "Keystone Division," as it was formed from units of the Pennsylvania Army National Guard. During World War II, it acquired the nickname the "Bloody Bucket" division by German forces due to its red insignia. But today the 28th infantry division goes by the name given to it by General

Hand Truck owned by the Boalsburg Fire Company

Pershing during World War I: the "Iron Division." The 28th is one of the most decorated infantry divisions in the United States Army.

In 1881, industrialist Andrew Carnegie bought 400 acres of land and took a 99 year lease on about 300 more acres from Moses Thompson, four miles west of State College in the area known as the Pine Barrens. His interest in the area was focused on iron ore. He used this naturally occurring mineral to make steel in his mills in Pittsburgh. The area where his mine was once located is now the Scotia Shooting Range which the PA Game Commission maintains for public use.

Initially, the closest rail station to the mine at Scotia was in Julian, and the first several thousand tons of iron ore were carted over rough roads to the rail line in Julian by mule-driven carts. Due to its proximity to the Pennsylvania Railroad, the mine got off to a good start. Later, Carnegie built a railroad from the mine to Julian. This railroad was eventually connected to the main line of the Pennsylvania Railroad, and it took 250 tons of Patton Township iron ore each day to steel mills in Pittsburgh.

Sometime about 1890, Andrew Carnegie saw that the iron ore from the Scotia mines was quickly being depleted and he lost interest in the area. Carnegie sold the Scotia mining operation in 1899 to the Bellefonte Furnace Company which operated it until 1909.

The town of Scotia was built by Carnegie and was named for Carnegie's homeland of Scotland. Scotia was a bustling mining town of some 400 people, complete with a school, a church, and even a civic center that housed a small library. The town grew from humble roots into a fine place to live. On summer nights, the town's baseball team would provide recreation for the people, and the town's band, the Forest Cornet Band, would provide entertainment. But by 1911, Scotia was a ghost town. The town has long since suffered the same fate as many other small logging and mining towns that once dotted central Pennsylvania.

In 1892, the Boalsburg Fire Company was established. Col. Theodore Boal is given credit for its organization. A hand truck was purchased from the State College Fire Company. The fire company was supported periodically by the Woman's Civic Club of Boalsburg.

The stock market crash of 1893 almost assured that the three villages would not recover in the near term. In 1880s, the Boalsburg Academy closed. Around the end of the century, the tannery in Boalsburg also closed.

The first water company in Boalsburg was organized in 1897. Water was obtained from a spring on Murray Mountain. It sufficed until the citizenry decided they wanted to add baths to their homes.

The Spanish American War was fought in 1898. Teddy Roosevelt charged up San Juan Hill to the cry of "Remember the Maine." As a result of this war, America took possession of Puerto Rico, the Philippines, and Guam. It was the first war America fought entirely on foreign soil.

The period 1855-1913 was one of vast change. The three villages would never be the same as they had been just 50 years earlier. The car and truck, the train, and the airplane are but a few of the things that altered everyday lives.

Economic Crisis of 1893

The Panic of 1893 was one of the worst stock market crashes in US history. It was also one of the most serious economic depressions in the country. It deeply affected every sector of the economy. It brought about panic, stock prices declined drastically, about 500 banks closed, 15,000 businesses failed, and many farms stopped operating. The unemployment rate in Pennsylvania rose to about 25 percent. The economy did not begin to recover until 1897. Clearly it was a bad crash.

Difficult Times

Beginning with the "Panic of 1837," Boalsburg and the surrounding area experienced difficult times. The stagecoach ceased operating circa 1855. According to the map by Tilden, by 1861, there was only one industrial mill (Rye Ho Woolen Factory) along

Spring Creek through Oak Hall-Dale's Mills. The area supported two sawmills and five gristmills. But by 1974, there was the woolen mill, no saw mills, and only two gristmills. In 1874, there were several small businesses, like blacksmith shops, quarries, and small furnaces, but nothing that would support a sizable workforce.

Since the beginning of the 19th century, the area's economy had largely been based on wagon traffic. With the "Panic of 1837," things began to change. With the end of the" Panic" conditions did not improve. The major reasons can be attributed to the Industrial Revolution which was largely responsible for the Oak Hall-Dale's Mills mill closings, the coming of the railroad which forced closure of the stagecoach, and later in the century, the automobile and truck. Standardized parts, steam power, and electricity made mass production and assembly lines possible, which led to a diminishing need for blacksmiths, carriage shops, and foundries. Many closed. Mass production techniques further doomed the regional economy.

The consequences of these difficult times were businesses closing their doors, fewer artisan and craftsmen, and declining or stagnant population growth. The logging industry seriously declined as ridges were stripped bare. The region of circa 1830 and the one of the early 1900s were vastly different.

TUMULTUOUS YEARS 1914-1975

By the turn of the century, the economy of the region was mainly reliant on agriculture. The tannery was closed. The tannery was one of the last links to the beginnings of Boalsburg. Centre Furnace was closed, the stagecoach was no longer operational, and most of the craftsmen and artisans, like coopers, tinsmiths, and hatters were either gone or were no longer in business. Most of the mills and a number of other businesses in Boalsburg, Oak Hall, and Linden Hall were out of business. By 1930, the blacksmith and carriage shops would be gone. Earlystown, Dale's Mills, and Rock Hill were gone as uniquely identifiable hamlets.

Some of the notable local events occurring during the period 1914-1975 are:
1914—Electricity comes to Boalsburg
1919—Columbus Chapel opens
1929—Sherm Lutz opens an air depot in Boalsburg
Circa 1930—West Penn Power Co. begins bringing electricity to the region
1933—The original Evangelical Church building in Linden Hall is dismantled
1934—Boalsburg Tavern burns
1937—Boalsburg High School is built

1937—The third Rock Hill/Linden Hall school closes
1938—Sherm Lutz is the first to deliver mail by air
1938—Egg Hill Church closes
1939—The lower school in Oak Hall closes
1948—The Irwin gristmill in Oak Hall closes
1966—State College Area School District is formed
1968—Nearly a third of Oak Hall disappears as the Pennsylvania Department of Highways (now PennDOT) builds the State College bypass
1972—The L&T Railroad ceases operation

During the next 63 years from 1914 through 1975, the three-village region was largely quiet. Little in the way of growth happened. America fought four foreign wars, the Spanish Influenzas pandemic meant there were few and poorly attended social and public events and empty streets most of the time, and a stock market crash which led to the Great Depression meant that church and government leaders had little time to consider growth issues. The population stagnated or dwindled.

In 1910, Meyer Dairy Farm commissioned Wheeland Bros. Carriage Shop in Boalsburg to build a horse-drawn milk wagon. It was probably one of the last such carriages built by a carriage shop in Boalsburg. With the coming of electricity, electric motors, lathes,

The Meyer Dairy carriage, 1910

etc., more and more items were made using standardized parts and components. Standardization made assembly lines practical. On the local level, standardization and mass production meant there was a greatly decreased demand for carriage shops and blacksmith shops. Artisans and craftsmen, which dominated the 19th century landscape, disappeared.

Churches

In 1933, the Evangelical Church in Linden Hall was dismantled. The only likely remaining remnants in the area of the lineages of the Cedar Creek Church in Linden Hall are the Academy Building in Boalsburg, the Evangelical Methodist Church in Linden Hall, and the State College Presbyterian Church.

In 1938, Egg Hill Church closed. Hereafter, it is said to be haunted.

In 1957, the St. John's German Reformed Church and the Congregational Church merged to form the United Church of Christ. The Church in Boalsburg was renamed the St. John's United Church of Christ.

Schools

The Boalsburg high school was built in 1937. It later became the Boalsburg Elementary School. The State College Area School District was formed in 1966.

In 1937, the Rock Hill school in Linden Hall closed. The students were bused to Boalsburg. The lower Oak Hall school closed. The students were also bused to Boalsburg. The closing of the Oak Hall lower school in 1939 marked a milestone, as it was the end of one-room schoolhouses in the Boalsburg-Oak Hall-Linden Hall area.

Post Offices

The mail drops in Oak Hall and Linden Hall were discontinued. All mail to these two locations was distributed by the post office in Boalsburg.

Columbus Chapel

Col. Theodore Boal was involved in numerous companies that brought water, electricity, telephone, and public transportation to the region.

His wife was a distant relative of Christopher Columbus. She inherited artifacts of Christopher Columbus, and in 1919, Theodore Boal brought these artifacts from Spain to Boalsburg and set up the Columbus Chapel.

The Columbus Chapel

Electricity comes to the region

In July 1914 the Boalsburg Electric Company was formed. Thus, Boalsburg became a part of the surge in America that had begun to utilize technology to generate electricity. It was recognized by villagers in Boalsburg that small-scale hydro-power systems could capture the energy in flowing water and convert it into cheap, clean electricity. Following successful litigation with the State College Water Company over water rights, a small hydroelectric plant was constructed in close proximity to where the tannery had been

Power House of the Boalsburg Electric Company

located and just east of the Boalsburg Heritage Museum. The power generated was limited. Electricity was turned on around dusk and tuned off about 10:00 p.m.

In 1930, West Penn Power Co. purchased the Boalsburg Electric Co. and began delivering reliable 24-hour service to the region. Soon the entire region was able to listen to "fireside chats" on their new-fangled, electric-powered radios.

World War I (The Great War)

The First World War lasted from August 1914 until the final Armistice with Germany on November 11, 1918 (Armistice Day is now called Veterans Day). The United States entered the War in 1917 to make the world safe for democracy. The war caused the disintegration of four empires: Austro-Hungarian, German, Ottoman, and Russian. Additionally, the English Empire suffered irreparable damage. The war also brought about radical changes in the European and Middle Eastern geographic maps.

Twenty-one veterans of WWI are buried in the Boalsburg cemetery. As in the Civil War, the village of Boalsburg and surrounding villages suffered a comparatively large number of casualties. The high number of casualties in the region highlighted the Army's draftee assignment policy. A draftee was allowed to enlist with his hometown pals and be assigned to the same unit together. If that unit became engaged in a heavy firefight, a large number of casualties from the same locale could occur. This policy was changed before World War II. The Boal Machine Gun troop was part of the 28th division and served during the war.

Spanish Influenza

About half the battlefield deaths in the Great War were from diseases rather than battlefield wounds. The trenches were a highly susceptible environment for the spread of disease, and army medicine and hospitals were primitive compared to modern standards.

Diseases were not limited to soldiers. Before the Great War ended in Nov. 1918, the Spanish Influenza pandemic had already begun. By 1921, the pandemic had infected an estimated 500 million people worldwide—about one-third of the planet's population—and killed an estimated 20-50 million victims, including some 675,000 Americans.

In the Boalsburg area, there were an unknown number of deaths. During the pandemic, there was little interaction among the citizens for fear of contracting the deadly disease. Streets were deserted most of the time. Churches ceased to function in their normally accustomed manner.

The Great Depression

In 1917, as the United States entered World War I, President Woodrow Wilson instituted a temporary wartime prohibition on the production of alcoholic beverages in order to save grain for food. That same year, Congress submitted the 18th amendment to the Constitution to the states for ratification. The proposed amendment banned the manufacture, transportation and sale of intoxicating liquors. The amendment was ratified on January 29, 1919 and went into effect a year later. In Linden Hall, the 1790s practice of making whiskey was not likely renewed. Homemade whiskey was made in utmost secrecy, as violators of the 18th amendment were put in jail.

The high price of bootleg liquor meant that the nation's working class and poor were impacted far more during Prohibition than middle- or upper-class Americans. As the cost for law enforcement rose and as the jail and prison populations spiraled upward, support for Prohibition waned in the 1920s. In 1933, the 21st amendment to the Constitution was ratified, repealing the 18th amendment.

In October 1929, the stock market crashed and plunged the nation into a deep recession. Fortunes were lost. The recession quickly spread to other industrialized countries and led to the Great Depression. It lasted until about 1939. It was the longest and most severe economic depression ever experienced by the industrialized countries of the Western world.

During the next three years, stock prices in the United States continued to plummet, until by late 1932 they had dropped to about 20 percent of their value in 1929. Besides ruining many thousands of individual investors, this precipitous decline in the value of assets greatly strained banks and other financial institutions. Many banks were forced into insolvency. Eleven thousand of the United States' 25,000 banks failed. The failure of so many banks, combined with a nationwide loss of confidence in the economy, led to much-reduced levels of spending and demand, and hence of production, thus aggravating the downward spiral. The result was drastically falling output and drastically rising unemployment. By 1932, U.S. manufacturing output had fallen to 54 percent of its 1929 level, and unemployment had risen to between 12 and 15 million workers, or 25-30 percent of the work force. It was not uncommon for a homeless man to be heard knocking at the door asking if he could do some odd job in exchange for a meal.

The Great Depression had a particular impact on farming communities like the Boalsburg, Oak Hall, and Linden Hall area that were dependent almost entirely on agriculture for their economic survival. The economic situation was exacerbated by the disastrous farming policies of the Roosevelt administration. The U.S. economy in the 1920s had experienced rapid economic growth and financial excesses. It became clear that there had been serious overproduction in agriculture, leading to falling prices and a rising debt among farmers.

As banks struggled for survival, many banks began to foreclose on small family farms. Many farmers quit farming and moved to industrial centers in search of jobs. The three village area was not immune to this situation.

In 1929, Sherm Lutz opened an air depot in Boalsburg atop the hill between Boalsburg and Oak Hall where "the pine tree" stood. He was the first to deliver the mail via air in 1938.

On Valentine's Day in 1934, the Boalsburg Tavern burned. The entire second floor and much of the first floor was destroyed. It was later determined that the cause of the fire was a defective flue. The burned out building stood dormant for three years. The building was eventually sold for $500 and restored by Ms. Billy Winsor. It was reopened in 1938.

Construction of the Pennsylvania Turnpike also began in 1938. The Turnpike was built in sections, and it was not finished until 1956, with the completion of the Delaware River Bridge, that one could travel from New Jersey to Ohio completely on the Turnpike. But from the outset, cross-state traffic began to migrate to this southern route, and soon there would be few cross-state travelers passing through the Boalsburg-Oak Hall-Linden Hall region.

World War II

In September 1939, Germany invaded Poland and prompted Great Britain and France to declare war on Germany, and World War II had begun. The U.S. entered the conflict in 1941. Germany surrendered in May 1945 and Japan surrendered in August 1945.

World War II proved to be the most devastating international conflict in history, taking the lives of some 35 to 60 million people, including 6 million Jews who died at the hands of the Nazis. Millions more were injured, and still more lost their homes and property. The legacy of the war would include the spread of communism from the Soviet Union into eastern Europe as well as its eventual triumph in China and a global shift in power from Europe to two rival superpowers, the United States and the Soviet Union, that would soon face off against each other in the Cold War.

Fifty veterans of WWII from the area are buried in the Boalsburg cemetery. The cemetery has veterans from every war the United States has ever fought, through the Vietnam War.

In 1941, scientists from Cambridge University in the United Kingdom and from the U.S. Department of Agriculture developed a low-cost way to mass produce penicillin, thereby saving many lives.

The Berlin Airlift, Berlin, Germany

Berlin Airlift

Following World War II, there were two superpowers, the United States and the Soviet Union. There was a constant struggle between the two for world influence and dominance. The struggle to deter the spread of communism is referred to as the Cold War.

The Berlin Blockade (24 June 1948 – 12 May 1949) was the first major international crisis of the Cold War. During the multinational occupation of post-World War II Germany, the Soviet Union blocked the Western Allies' railway, road, and canal access to the sectors of Berlin under Allied control. Their aim was to force the western powers to allow the Soviet zone to start supplying Berlin with food, fuel, and aid, thereby giving the Soviets practical control over the entire city of Berlin. In response, the Western Allies organized the Berlin Airlift to carry supplies to the people in West Berlin. Aircrews from the United States Air Force, the British Royal Air Force, the Royal Canadian Air Force, the Royal Australian Air

Force, the Royal New Zealand Air Force, and the South African Air Force flew over 200,000 flights in one year, providing up to 4,700 tons of necessities daily, such as fuel and food, to the Berliners.

By the spring of 1949 the effort was clearly succeeding, and by April the airlift was delivering more cargo than had previously been transported into the city by rail. The success of the Berlin Airlift brought embarrassment to the Soviets, who had refused to believe the airlift could make a difference. The blockade was lifted in May 1949 and resulted in the creation of two separate German states. Germany was divided into the Federal Republic of Germany (West Germany) and the German Democratic Republic (East Germany).

Korean War

On June 25, 1950, the Korean War began when some 75,000 soldiers from the North Korean People's Army poured across the 38th parallel, the boundary between the Soviet-backed Democratic People's Republic of Korea to the north and the pro-Western Republic of Korea to the south. This invasion was the first bona fide military action of the Cold War. By July 1950, American troops had entered the war on South Korea's behalf. As far as American officials were concerned, it was a war against the forces of international communism. In July 1953, the Korean War came to an end. In all, some 5 million soldiers and civilians lost their lives during the war. Four Korea War veterans are buried in the Boalsburg cemetery.

Cuban Missile Crisis

The Cuban Missile Crisis was a 13-day (October 16–28, 1962) confrontation between the United States and the Soviet Union initiated after the American discovery of Soviet ballistic missile deployment in Cuba.

Partly in response to the presence of American Jupiter ballistic missiles in Italy and Turkey, Soviet leader Nikita Khrushchev agreed to Cuba's request to place nuclear missiles on the island to deter a future invasion. An agreement was reached during a secret meeting between Khrushchev and Fidel Castro in July 1962, and construction of a number of missile launch facilities started later that summer.

The missile preparations were confirmed when an Air Force U-2 spy plane produced clear photographic evidence of medium-range and intermediate-range ballistic missile facilities. The United States established a naval blockade on October 22 to prevent further missiles from reaching Cuba. The United States announced that it

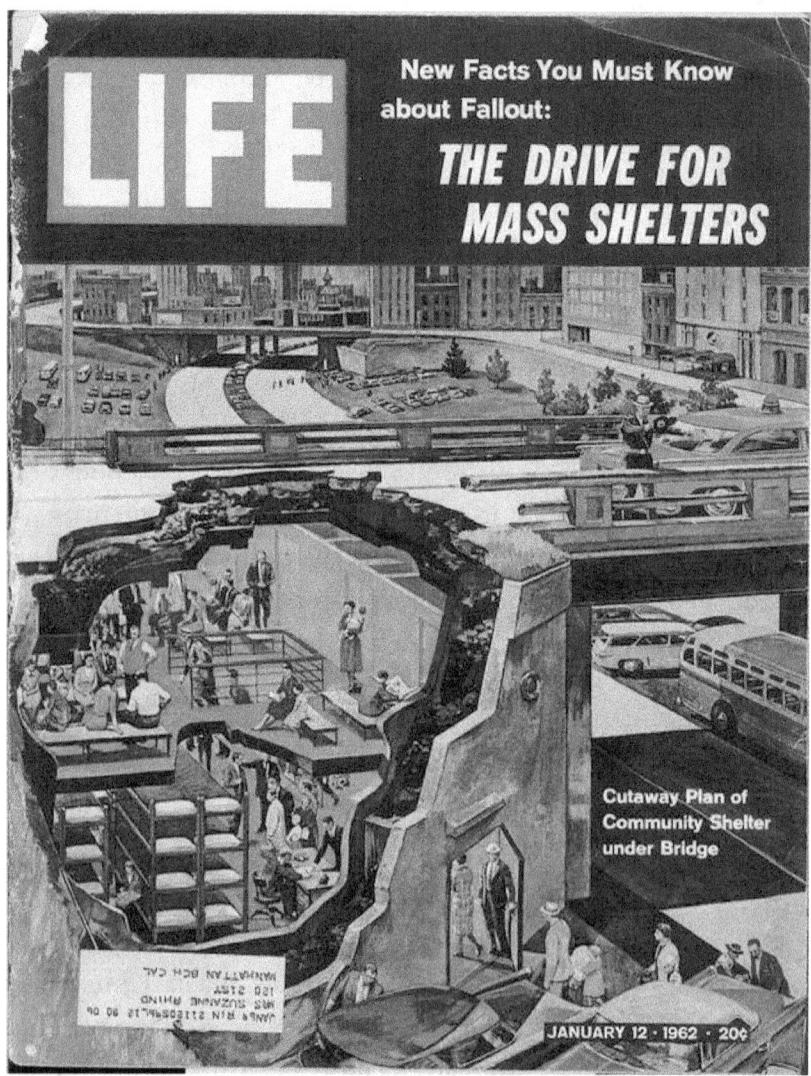

Life Magazine *spread on fallout shelters*

would not permit offensive weapons to be delivered to Cuba and demanded that the weapons already in Cuba had to be dismantled and returned to the Soviet Union.

After several days of tense negotiations, an agreement was reached between U.S. President John Kennedy and Khrushchev. The Soviets would dismantle their offensive weapons in Cuba and return them to the Soviet Union in exchange for a U.S. declaration and agreement not to invade Cuba. Further, the United States agreed that it would dismantle all U.S.-built Jupiter missiles which had been deployed in Turkey against the Soviet Union.

When all offensive missiles and light bombers had been withdrawn from Cuba, the blockade was formally ended on November 21, 1962.

With the end of World War II and the start of the Cold War, the United States had grown concerned about the expansion of communism. A Latin American country openly allying with the Soviet Union was regarded by the United States as unacceptable. It would, for example, defy the Monroe Doctrine, which was a U.S. policy limiting U.S. involvement in European colonies and European affairs but holding that the Western Hemisphere was in the exclusive U.S. sphere of influence.

The Cuban Missile Crisis was but one in a number of confrontations between the United States and the Soviet Union during the Cold War. However, it is considered the closest the two adversaries ever came to hostilities escalating into a full-scale nuclear war.

The Cuban Missile Crisis was a scary time in U.S. history. All across the United States, bomb shelters were established. Many citizens built private shelters.

Vietnam War

The Vietnam War was an undeclared war in Vietnam, Laos, and Cambodia from 1 November 1955 to the fall of Saigon on 30 April 1975. It was officially fought between North Vietnam and South Vietnam. North Vietnam was supported by the Soviet Union, China, and other communist allies. South Vietnam was supported by the United States, South Korea, the Philippines, Australia, Thailand, and other anti-communist allies. It lasted some 19 years, with direct U.S. involvement ending in 1973 following the Paris Peace Accords, and included the Laotian Civil War and the Cambodian Civil War, resulting in all three countries becoming communist states in 1975.

American military advisors began arriving in what was then French Indochina in 1950. After the French quit Indochina in 1954, the United States assumed financial and military responsibility for the South Vietnamese state. By 1964, there were 23,000 U.S. troops in Vietnam, but this escalated further following a 1964 incident in which a U.S. destroyer was allegedly attacked by a North Vietnamese fast attack craft in the Gulf of Tonkin. Thereafter, troop levels increased to 184,000.

Gradual withdrawal of U.S. ground forces began as part of a "Vietnamization" program, which aimed to end American involvement in the war. Direct U.S. military involvement ended on 15 August 1973. The capture of Saigon by North Vietnamese forces in April 1975 marked the end of the war, and North and South Vietnam were reunified the following year.

The war exacted a huge human cost in terms of fatalities. Estimates of the number of Vietnamese soldiers and civilians killed vary from 966,000 to 3.8 million. Some 275,000–310,000 Cambodians, 20,000–62,000 Laotians, and 58,220 U.S. service members also died in the conflict, and a further 1,626 remain missing in action.

Within the United States the war gave rise to what was referred to as Vietnam Syndrome, an aversion to American overseas military involvement, which together with Watergate contributed to the crisis of confidence that affected America throughout the 1970s.

State College Bypass

In 1968, disaster struck the village of Oak Hall. The Pennsylvania Department of Highways took the upper third of the village to construct the State College bypass. Today, the upper third of the village is a traffic interchange. Buildings were destroyed and Spring Creek was rerouted.

The Quiet Villages
Not much of significance happened in the three villages during the period 1915-1970. During this period, the United States fought four wars, fought off a pandemic, and there was the Great Depression. Additionally, there was the Cold War. Political and church leaders alike had little opportunity to contemplate growth issues.

Resurgence
By the early 1970s, the three villages had suffered through a lengthy period where there had been minimal sources of outside income coming into the villages. There were few shops and stores, no industries, or few businesses. Many residences were in need of repair with limited funds available. It was a relatively low period in the history of Boalsburg, Oak Hall, and Linden Hall.

It was at this time that The Pennsylvania State University decided that the future direction of the university was as a world-class teaching and research institution. The university expansion that followed led to a new era of growth in and around State College. Increased business opportunities brought more residents to the area. University expansion brought in more faculty and staff. Many settled in the Boalsburg-Oak Hall-Linden Hall vicinity, creating more business opportunities and began revitalizing the area.

LOOKING BACKWARD AND LOOKING FORWARD

During its 200-plus year history there have been many prominent leaders of Boalsburg, Oak Hall, and Linden Hall that were largely responsible for the growth and development of the area. Among these were John and James Irwin, Daniel Hess, and the Boal family. Most served in the state legislature and the U.S. Congress. Additionally, the three-village area is home to three U.S. ambassadors. The first Ambassador was William Irvin, son of John Irvin of Linden Hall and brother of General James of Oak Hall. He was Ambassador to Amboy (now called China) in 1864. The next Ambassador was Cyrus E. Woods who served as Ambassador to Japan around 1900. Pierre de Lagarde Boal, son of Theodore Boal, was Ambassador to Bolivia and Nicaragua. He earlier held diplomatic posts in Canada, Mexico, Yugoslavia, Poland, Switzerland, and Peru. There have been many unnamed individuals who have contributed mightily to the health and well-being of the area.

The evolution of Boalsburg, Oak Hall, and Linden Hall can generally be traced by tracking churches and schoolhouses. For instance, with the exception of the Evangelical Methodist Church in Linden Hall (1897), no new churches have been built in the three villages since 1868. The lack of activity in Boalsburg and Oak Hall coincides with the full effect of the Industrial Revolution at the end of the 19th century and the distressful events throughout the 20th century.

The church in Linden Hall was built during the brief economic revival stimulated by the logging operations.

New schools have been built in all three villages as replacement structures for older schools. The opening of new schools has sometimes coincided with the closing of others.

Around 1800, the three villages began a period of growth. Numerous mills were built in Oak Hall along Spring Creek. Some mills produced finished goods like woolen garments and hemp rope, while others produced raw products. The area supported gristmills and flour mills, iron furnaces, iron ore pits, and quarries. The outside income made the villages very prosperous. The road network made the area a gateway through Potter's Mills, down Seven Mountains, and on to eastern markets. The volume of wagon traffic led to many small businesses that catered to the wagoneers. These included blacksmiths, tanners, carriage shops, and taverns/inns. This activity attracted local and cross-state stagecoach business. The stagecoach business further attracted tinsmiths, hatters, seamstresses, boot makers, and more. The three-village area was an important center of commerce. The high-water mark for the area, economically speaking, was around 1830-1840.

By the end of the 19th century, the situation had changed dramatically. The stagecoach had ceased operation, and Centre Furnace had closed. Most of the mills in Oak Hall were closed, too. While the railroad and logging gave Linden Hall a reprieve in the latter part of the 19th century, it was only a brief period of prosperity. The primary culprit for the region's eventual downfall, broadly speaking, was the Industrial Revolution.

The wagon traffic through the area had been reduced, and the railroad had isolated the village. Many of the craftsmen and artisans had either died, were out of business, or had gone elsewhere. The tannery closed and the carriage shops and blacksmith shops would only survive a short time into the 20th century. The only thing that remained from the first half of the 19th century was agriculture.

The 120 years from 1856 to 1975 were turbulent ones. The area was increasingly influenced by national and international events. The region has had to rely almost exclusively on an agricultural economy.

From 1856 to 1975, the region experienced six wars. Throughout this time, the residents of the three villages and Harris Township always supported the military, despite having 133 of its young men who were war veterans buried in the Boalsburg cemetery. Additional distress was caused by the Industrial Revolution, the Spanish Influenza pandemic, two stock market crashes, and the Great Depression. The leaders of the region had few opportunities to focus on growth or development issues.

The economic downturn of the region in the 19th century did not take full effect until after the Civil War. There were several indications of economic distress late in the 19th century. In the 20th century, the main causes were the numerous wars and the Great Depression.

Throughout history, there has always been interaction between the Boalsburg, Oak Hall, and Linden Hall communities. Early interaction took place at "the pine tree" meeting place. Many residents of Oak Hall and Linden Hall attended church at Old Stone Church and are buried in the Boalsburg Cemetery. There were common places of work, and friendships were undoubtedly made. Many paths crossed at the Boalsburg post office. Today, the opportunities for interaction abound at church, the post office, and through numerous organizations.

The future looks promising for the Boalsburg-Oak Hall-Linden Hall communities. Today, the villages have evolved into bedroom communities for State College and Penn State University. The economy has changed from one based on small industry and business to one largely based on agriculture. Additional income also comes in as a result of tourism.

The Boal Mansion and Columbus Chapel are being revitalized and continue to attract visitors from out of town. The Memorial Day celebration, People's Choice Festival, and Hometown Christmas bring in many visitors that provide valuable support for local small businesses. Many other visitors contribute to the local economy during the Penn State football season. Harris Township is one of the fastest-growing townships in the region.

BIBLIOGRAPHY

Centre County Historical Society. *Up, Up and Away: Sherm Lutz and the State College Air Depot.* Centre County Historical Society, 2019.

Chernow, Ron. *Titan—The Life of John D. Rockefeller.* Vintage Books, New York, NY, 2004.

Correspondence with Virginia Rainey of the Huntingdon Presbytery, Sept. 27, 2019.

Corter, R. *A Story of Harris Township Schools.* Boalsburg Heritage Museum.

Corter, R. H. and M. T. Riley. *Boalsburg—An American Village.* Boalsburg Village Conservancy, Boalsburg, PA, 1986. 36 pp.

Eggert, G. G. *Making Iron on the Bald Eagle—Roland Curtin's Ironworks and Worker's Community.* Centre County Historical Society, State College, PA, 2000.

Horner, C. *The History of Boalsburg Tavern—and the Woman Who Saved It.* The Centre County Historical Society, State College, PA, 2019.

Linden Hall Garden Club. *Linden Hall Roller Mills.* Centre County Historical Society, State College, PA, Circa 1960.

Linn, J. B. *History of Centre and Clinton Counties*, Pennsylvania, Centre County Historical Society, 1883.

Magargel, Myrtle. *History of Boalsburg.* Centre Daily Times/Boalsburg Heritage Museum, 1938.

McElhoe, Janice S. *Village Craftsmen: Boalsburg Artisans in the 1800s.* Boalsburg Heritage Museum, 2015, 39 pp.

Mitchell, J. Thomas . *Centre County: From Its Earliest Settlement to the Year 1915*, Pennsylvania State University Libraries, 1915.

Murry, Augusta E. *The Pine Tree, Nothing More.* Boalsburg, Pa. 1 pp.

Nichols, B. *Atlas of Centre County*. Pomeroy & Co., Philadelphia, PA, 1874.

Rainey, Virginia. *Around the Synod, Hunting Presbytery*, Huntingdon, PA, Jan. 12, 2017.

Ricker, Dennis and Beth Ricker. *Daniel Hess: a Pioneer Country Merchant at Linden Hall*. Linden Hall Village Association, 1988.

Rishel, Ruth E. *Potter Township: General Potter's Empire*. Centre Hall-Potter Township Bicentennial Project, 1976.

Shortess, J. D., and A. D. Gramley. *History of the Central Pennsylvania Conference of the Evangelical Church*. Evangelical Press, Harrisburg, PA (1940).

Thomas, Michael J. *Centre County: From Its Earliest Settlement to the Year 1915*, Pennsylvania State University Libraries, 1915.

Tilden, S, D. *Atlas of Centre County*. Pomeroy & Co. Philadelphia, PA, 1861.

Van Tries, Thomas C. *The Presbytery of Huntingdon—West Penns-Valley Church*. Democratic Watchman, Bellefonte, PA, September 26, 1902.

White, R. C. *American Ulysses—A Life of Ulysses S. Grant*. Random House, New York, NY, 2017.

www.centrehistory.org/centre-countys-townships-and-boroughs

www.en.wikipedia.org/wiki/Sawmill

www.historicmapworks.com/Map/US/12353/Harris++Boalsburg/Centre+County+1874/Pennsylvania/

www.keytometals.com/fluxana/page.aspx?ID=CheckArticle&site=kts&NM=106

www.livingplaces.com/PA/Centre_County/College_Township/Felix_Dale_House.html

www.livingplaces.com/PA/Centre_County/College_Township/Oak_Hall_Historic_District.html

www.livingplaces.com/PA/Centre_County/Millheim_Borough/Millheim_Historic_District.html

www.millpictures.com/mills.php?millid=5021

www.syntrinity.org/synod/history-huntingdon-presbytery-rural-roots-still-shine-today/

www.thoughtco.com/significant-stages-american-industrial-revolution-4164132

www.en.wikipedia.org/wiki/Bessemer_process

www.en.wikipedia.org/wiki/Linden_Hall_Historic_District

www.en.wikipedia.org/wiki/Gristmill

APPENDIX A

MISCELLANEOUS MAPS

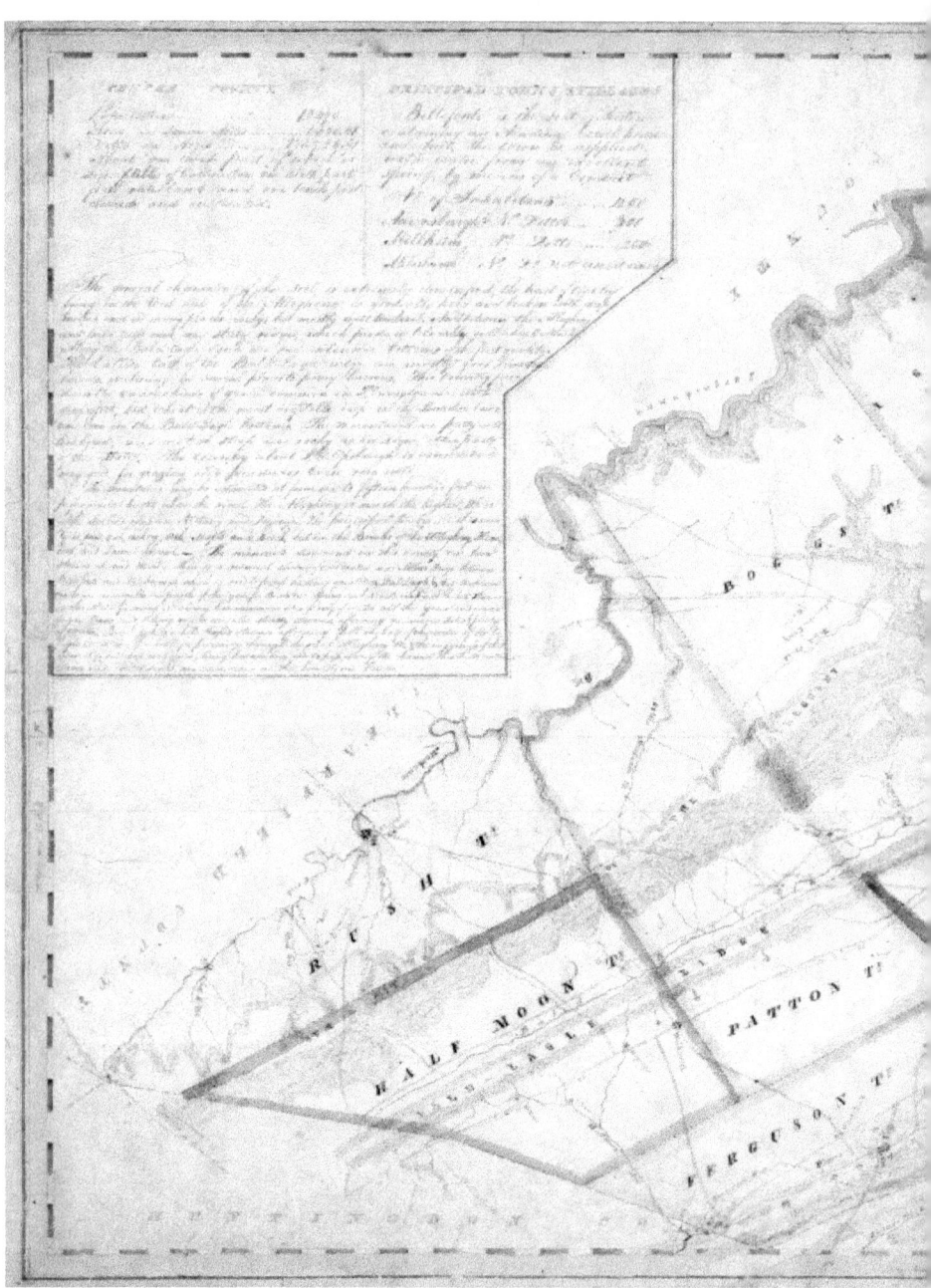

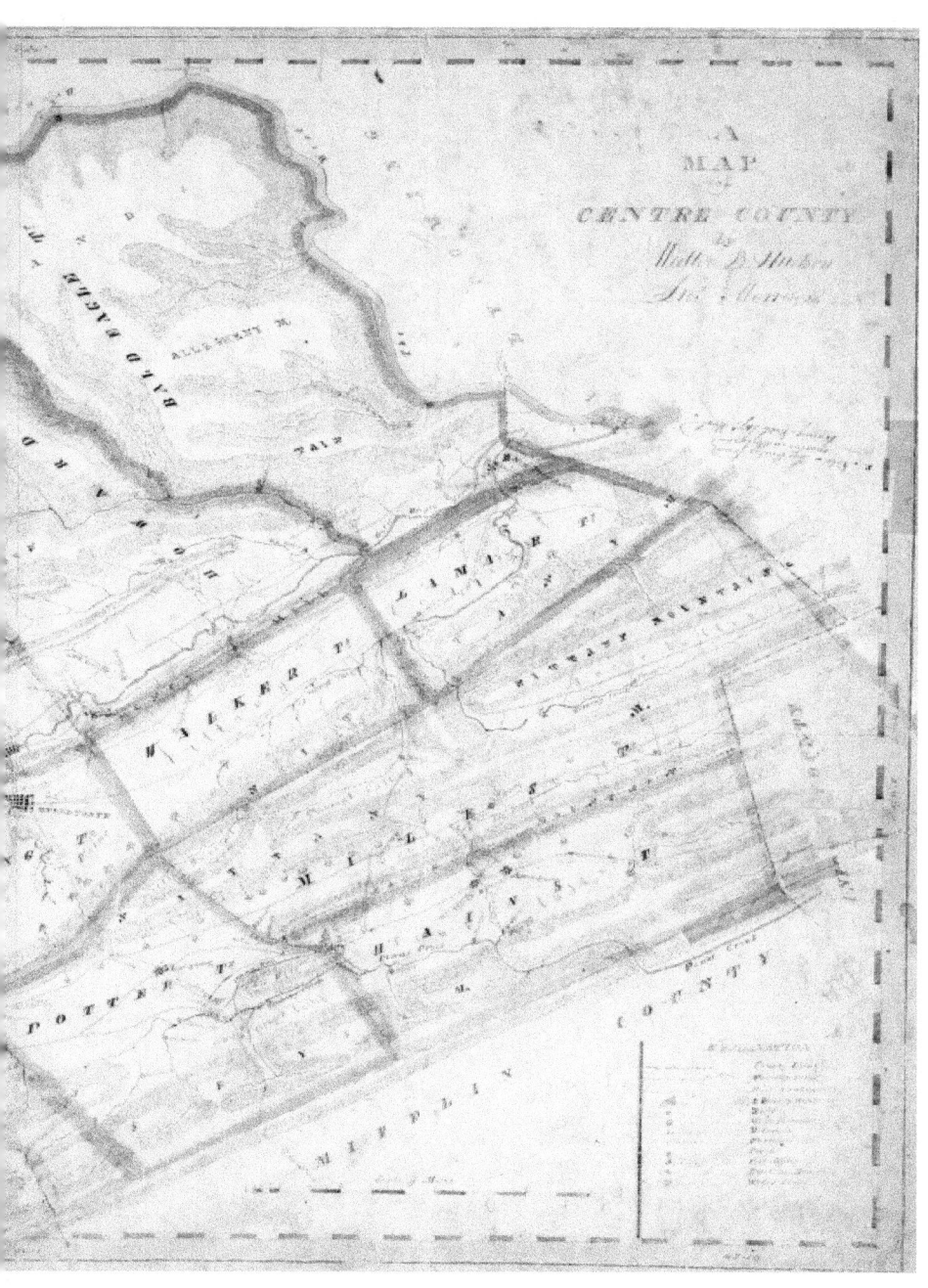

Whiteside Map of Centre County, 1822

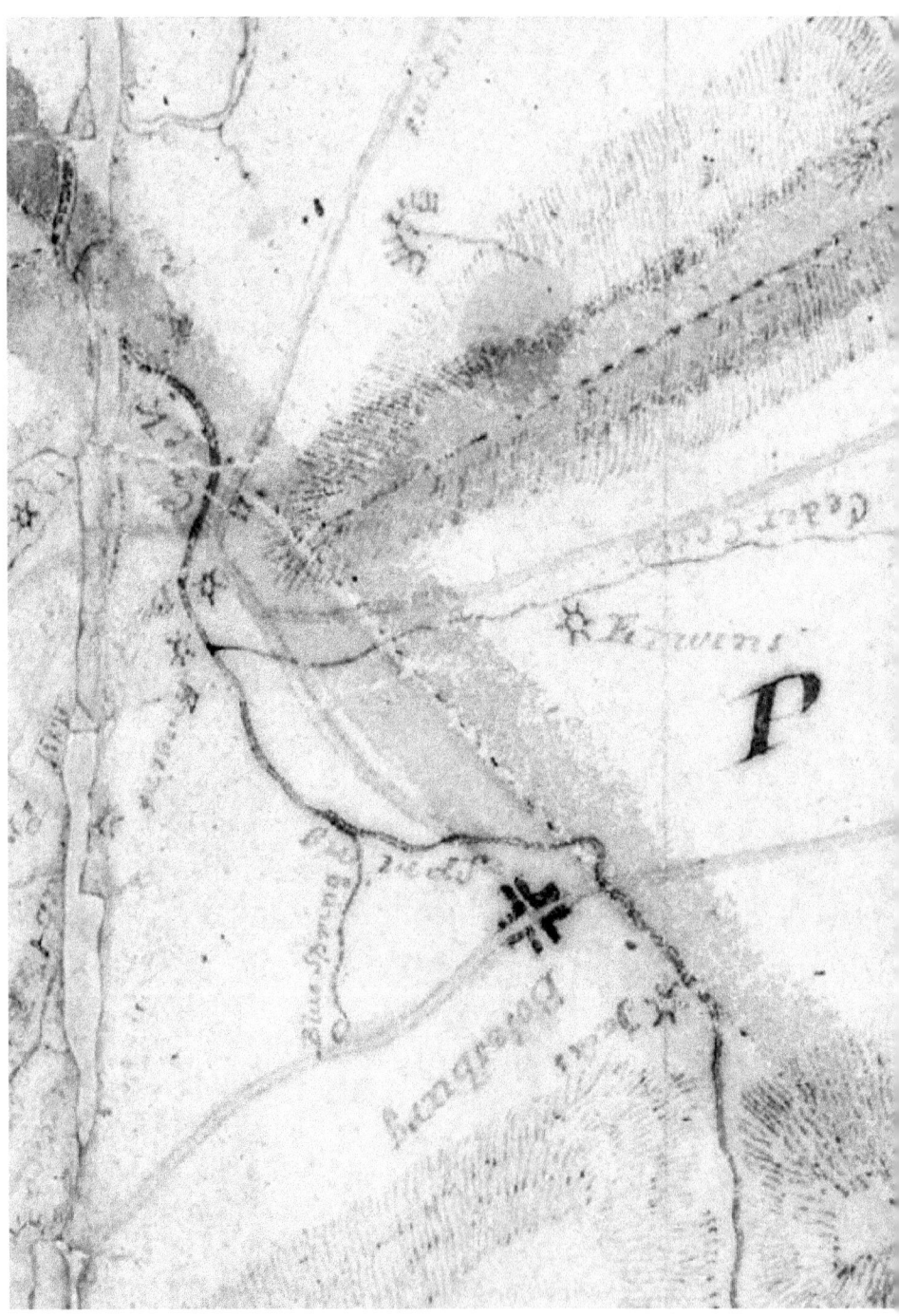

Insert of the Boalsburg region from Whiteside Map of Centre County, 1822.

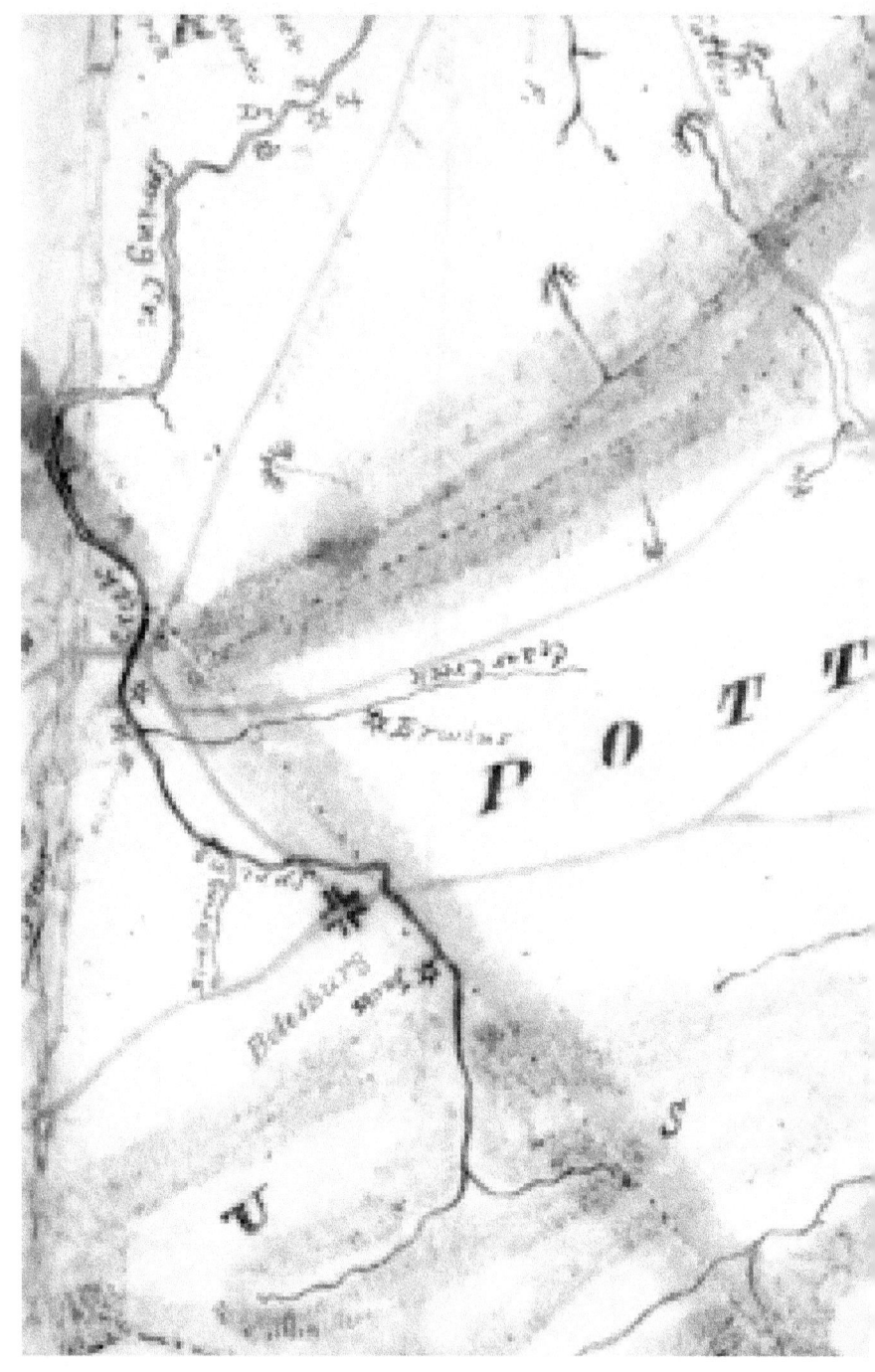

Insert of Potter Township (enhanced)
from Whiteside Map of Centre County, 1822

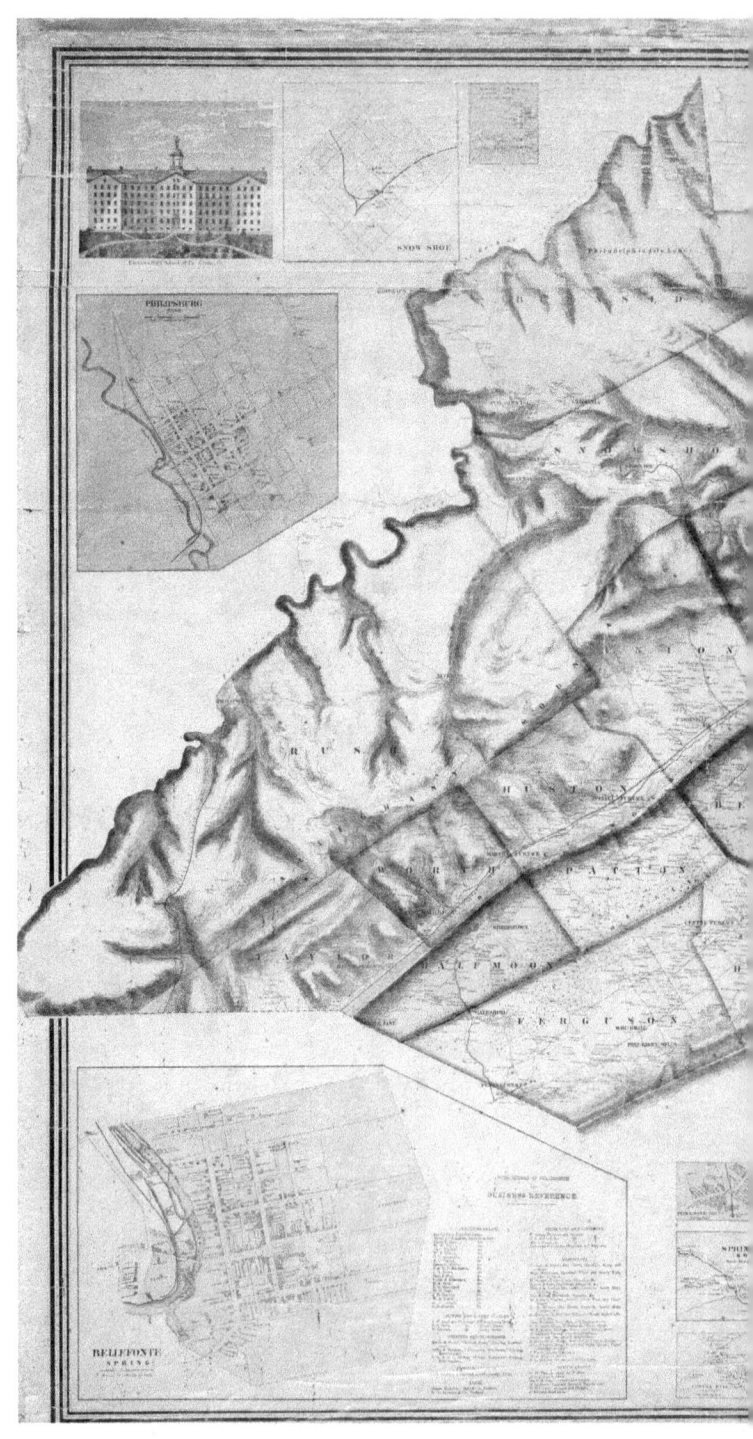

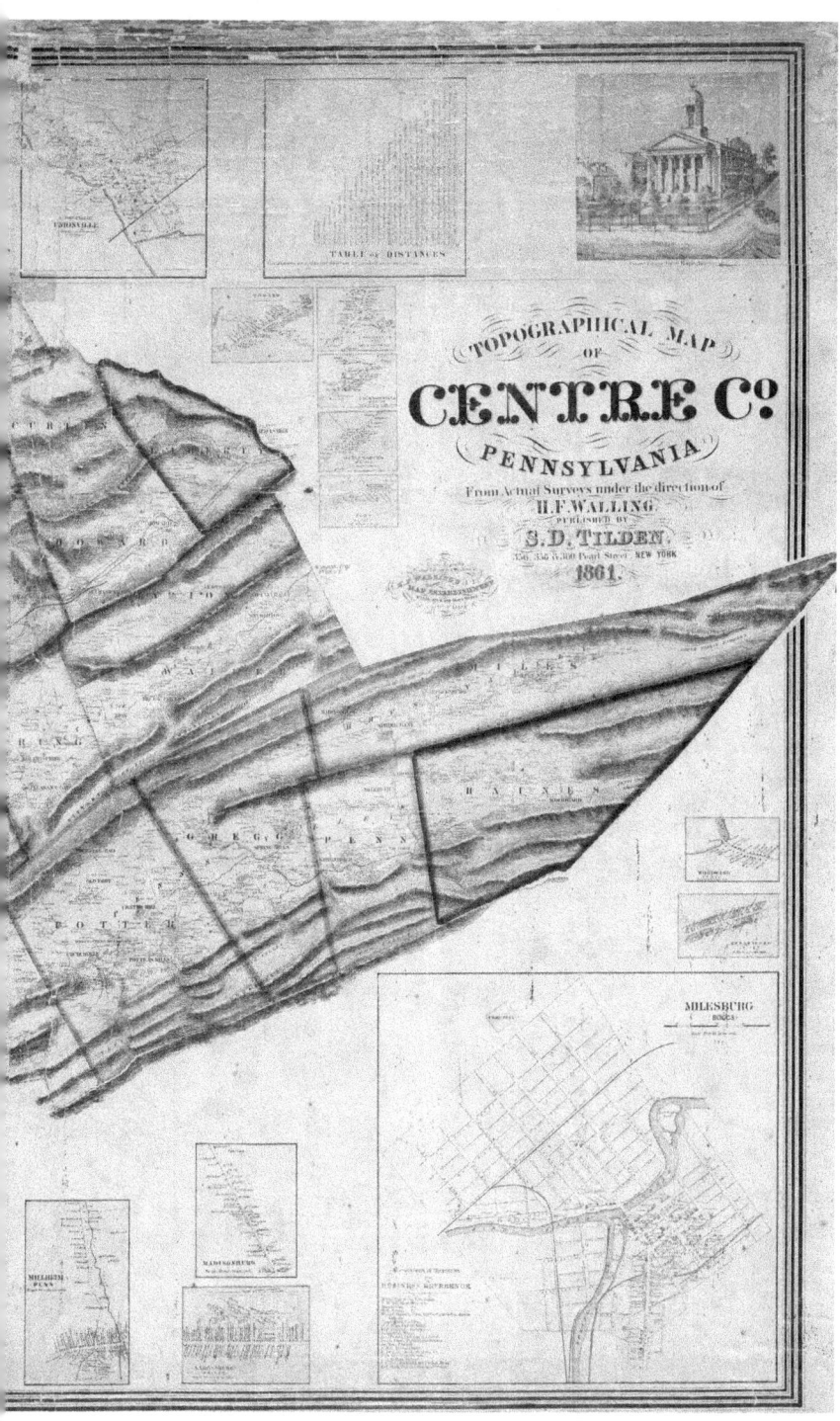

The 1861 Tilden Map of Centre County

Boalsburg-Oak Hall-Linden Hall
insert from the
1861 Tilden Map of Centre County

Boalsburg-Oak Hall-Linden Hall insert from the 1874 map of Centre County

Enhanced map of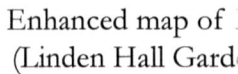
(Linden Hall Gardens)

```
            LEGEND
    —  present in 1890
    —  present in 1980
    —  present in both years
    ·  house
    -  barn
    *  commercial business
    +  church
    ○  pond
```

Boalsburg insert from 1874 Polmeroy Map

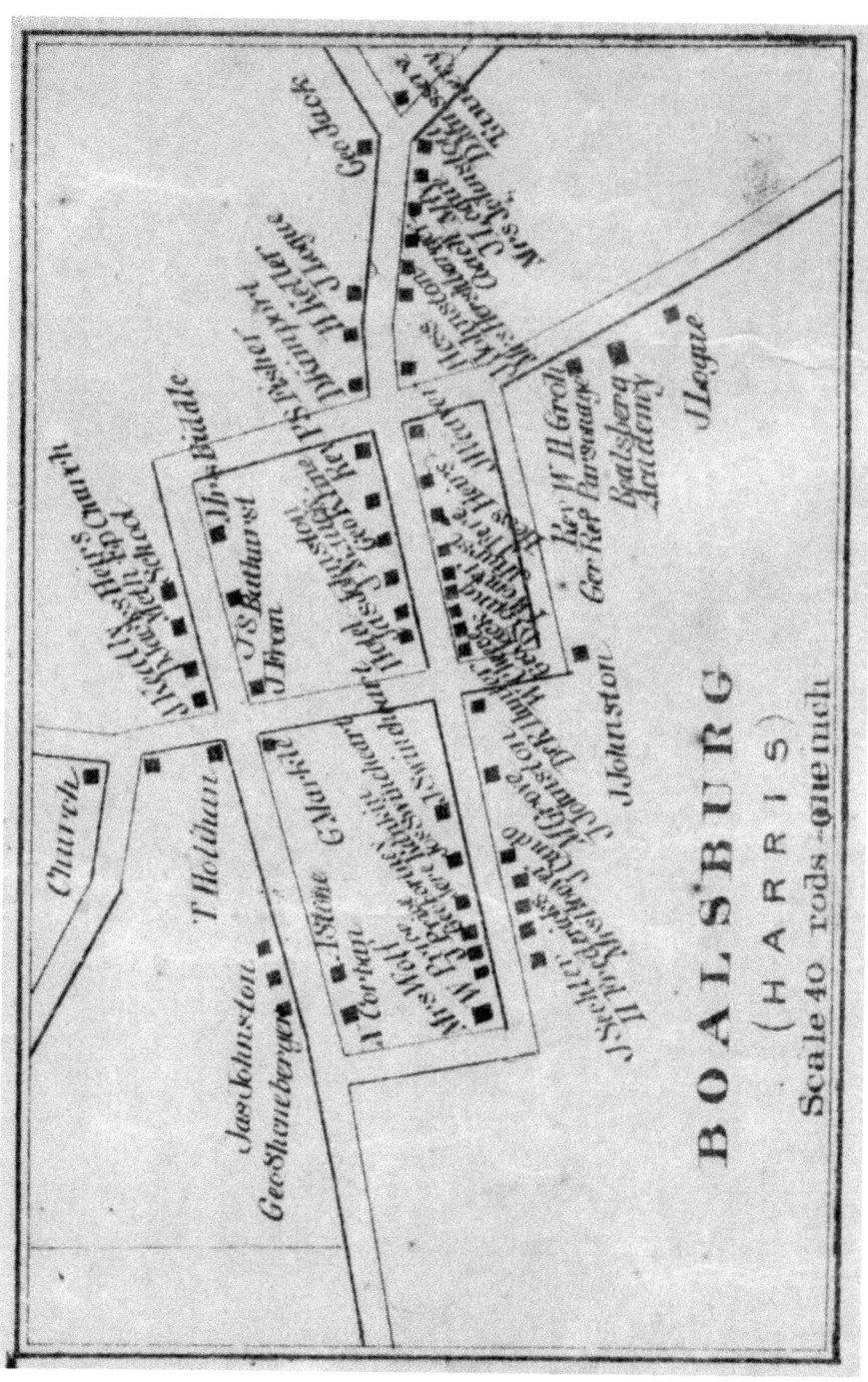

Boalsburg insert from 1861 Tilden Map

Potter Township (ca. 1900)

APPENDIX B
KEY TIMELINE DATES

1764—Gen. James Potter is the first to explore Centre County

1765—Centre County land office opens

1766—Thomas Poultney purchases Harmony Plantation in Springfield

1769—Andrew Boggs becomes the first white settler in Centre County

1774—Benjamin Poultney is the first settler in Springfield

1777—Gen. Potter builds Potter's Fort

Circa 1778—The "Great Runaway" to Fort Granville in Lewistown follows a reported incident involving American Indians in May 1778

1779—Cleary Campbell becomes one of the first settlers to return from Lewistown to Penns Valley following the "Great Runaway"

Circa 1785—Settlers begin returning to upper Penns Valley after the "Great Runaway"

1785—All American Indians have left Centre County

1789—James and Henry Whitehill settle in Oak Hall

1789—David Boal, Sr. moves to Springfield and builds the Boal Mansion

1790—Christian and Felix Dale move to Centre County

1792—Centre Furnace begins operation as the first business in Centre County

1794—John Irwin emigrates to Linden Hall

Circa 1795—The Springfield-Potter's Mills toll road and Boalsburg Pike are built, opening an alternate route to Potter's Mills and the eastern seaboard

Circa 1800—The Christian and Felix Dale build a gristmill and sawmill at what would become known as Dale's Mills.

Circa 1801—George McCormick builds a gristmill and sawmill at what would become known as Oak Hall

1802—The first Rock Hill School is built at Linden Hall

1804—David Boal, Jr. opens the Boal Tavern/inn in Springfield

Circa 1804—Stagecoach begins local operation connecting Springfield to Linden Hall

1808—John Irvin builds a gristmill in Linden Hall

1810—John Irwin completes building a brick home in Linden Hall

1810—Andrew Stroup lays out a plan for the village of Springfield

Circa 1810—The first schoolhouse in Springfield is built

1810—Curtin Iron Works near Bellefonte opens

Circa 1815—Cross-state travel via stagecoach is established

Circa 1815—A schoolhouse is built in upper Oak Hall

Circa 1818—Cottage industries emerge

1819—Boalsburg Tavern is built

1820—A new post office is established in Boalsburg

Circa 1820—The "Lewis and Connelly Gang" is elminated as a

menace to travelers passing through Seven Mountians

1822—The James Irwin brick mill in Oak Hall is built

1825—James Irwin completes building the Irwin mansion in Oak Hall

Circa 1820-1830—Numerous mills open for business in Oak Hall-Dale's Mills

1827—The constructiom of Zion Union Church (The Old Stone Church) brings two new churches from Oak Hall to Boalsburg

1830—The first Rock Hill/Linden Hall school burns down

1835—Harris Township is established

1837—The panic of 1837 begins

1840—The second Rock Hill/Linden Hall school is built

1853—Boalsburg Academy opens

1855—The Farmers' High School, which is now known as the Pennsylvania State University, opens

Circa 1855—Stagecoach ceases to operate

1858—The Centre Furnace closes for business

1862—St. John's German Reformed builds a new church in Boalsburg

1862—A mail drop is established in Linden Hall

1879—A schoolhouse in lower Oak Hall is built

1868—The Old Stone Church is demolished, making way for the Zion Lutheran Church

1879—The lower schoolhouse in Oak Hall is built

1885—The L&T Railroad comes to Linden Hall and Oak Hall

Circa 1885—Whitmer and Reitz Company begins logging in Bear Meadows

1885—Huyett and Livingood begins producing rail cars

Circa 1890—McCoy and Linn begin producing charcol for local iron furnaces

1886—A mail drop is established on the hill near the "pine tree" between Oak Hall and Boalsburg

1892—The Boalsburg Fire Company is organized

1893—Boalsburg Academy closes

1893—The second Rock Hill/Linden Hall school is demolished and replaced with the third Rock Hill/Linden Hall school

1895—Linden Hall Lumber Company moves to Linden Hall, sets up a sawmill ln the villge beside Cedar Run, and begins producing lumber

1897—The Boalsburg Water Company is established

1897—Evangelical Methodist Church is built in Linden Hall

1914—Electricity comes to Boalsburg

1919—Columbus Chapel opens

1929—Sherm Lutz opens an airfield in Boalsburg

Circa 1930—West Penn Power Co. begins bringing electricity to the region

1933—The original Evangelical Church building in Linden Hall is dismantled

1934—Boalsburg Tavern burns

1937—Boalsburg High School is built

1937—The third Rock Hill/Linden Hall school closes

1938—Sherm Lutz is the first the first to deliver mail by air

1939—The lower school in Oak Hall closes

1948—The Irwin gristmill in Oak Hall closes

1966—State College Area School District is formed

1968—Nearly a third of Oak Hall disappears as the Pennsylvania Department of Highways builds the State College bypass

1972—The L&T Railroad ceases operations

www.ingramcontent.com/pod-product-compliance
Lightning Source LLC
Chambersburg PA
CBHW070146080526
44586CB00015B/1867